COURTING

BUSINESS

101 Ways for *Accelerating* Business Relationships

COURTING

BUSINESS

101 Ways for *Accelerating* Business Relationships

Ann Marie Sabath

Author of *Business Etiquette*

CAREER
PRESS
Franklin Lakes, NJ

COURTING BUSINESS
EDITED BY GINA M. CHESELKA
TYPESET BY STACEY A. FARKAS
Cover design by Johnson Design
Printed in the U.S.A. by Book-mart Press

To order this title, please call toll-free 1-800-CAREER-1 (NJ and Canada: 201-848-0310) to order using VISA or MasterCard, or for further information on books from Career Press.

The Career Press, Inc., 3 Tice Road, PO Box 687, Franklin Lakes, NJ 07417
www.careerpress.com

Library of Congress Cataloging-in-Publication Data
Sabath, Ann Marie.
    Courting business : 101 ways for accelerating business relationships / by Ann Marie Sabath.
        p. cm.
    Includes index.
    ISBN 1-56414-769-X
    1. Success in business--Handbooks, manuals, etc. 2. Creative ability in business--Handbooks, manuals, etc. I. Title.

    HF5386.S22 2005
    650.1'3--dc22

                                                2004056560

Acknowledgments

My grateful thanks go out to:

That man of vision, my publisher, Ron Fry.

My parents, Mary and Camille Sabath, who taught me how the "power of nice" could take you far.

My assistant, Suzy, who went beyond the call of duty to help me with this book.

To Brandon Toropov, who continues to be a very important part of my writing team.

My editor, Gina Cheselka, for her infinite patience in getting this book into its final form.

Herb Liss, who invited me to his Managing the Entrepreneurial Venture class at Xavier University to address how to develop business relationships long before I knew I had anything to say about it.

Tom Swink and Dave Petersen, who invited me to be part of their Fifth Third Bank Regional Sales Blitz, which became the foundation for this topic.

Chena Dederian, who introduced me to her mother's "Stroke, Don't Provoke" concept.

Mr. Klekamp for sharing core business practices that readers of this book will find invaluable.

My June 27th friend, Laura Kozlowski, who taught me the "Ask, Don't Tell" principle.

Todd Jenkins, who taught me how to tune into the way auditory prospects do business.

My children, Scott and Amber, who are walking the talk of this book's courtship tips as they climb the slippery ladder of success in their careers.

My pooches, Micah and Daisy, who so loyally kept me company as I was writing this book.

Contents

Introduction

What Prompted This Book

The year was 2000. I had just started my 13th year in business. My banker called me and asked if we could meet for coffee.

I don't know about you, however when anyone from a financial institution asks me for a meeting, my antennae start twitching. What was this all about? Both my business and personal equity lines were with this bank. My debts had been paid in full for some time.

Did he know something I didn't? If so, what?

We arranged to get together the following morning. It was with some relief that I heard my banker say, "Ann Marie, I'd like you to speak at our Sales Blitz next month. I've watched you grow a lean and mean business on a shoestring budget, with a tiny staff. I'd like you to explain to our sales team what it takes to be successful."

Of course, I was stunned. *Moi*? Being asked to share my views on how to be successful with the rainmakers of the most profitable super-regional bank in the country?

Until that moment, I had never considered myself successful!

During the following weekend, I tried to figure out what I could possibly tell a group of savvy salespeople that they didn't already know. Ever since I launched my business in 1987, I had given it my all. I had acquired a strong work ethic and good values from watching my parents and grandparents. Like them, I took work very seriously.

Even though I owned my business, I had never played hooky from work (unless "hooky" was part of a scheduled vacation, of course).

One thing I realized that I *could* talk about was the values that drove my company. My team and I have maintained the philosophy that each and every client is extremely important to us.

What's more, we demonstrate our respect for them by consistently under-promising and over-delivering.

I also gave some thought to the systems that my team and I had in place for developing and accelerating business relationships. We simply do what it takes to get the job done. Period. Our workday is over when deadlines are met—and not before.

I also realized that no client or project was "too small" and that all our clients were given the same attention as the largest ones.

It occurred to me, too, that we did not take rejection personally and that we consistently followed up with prospects and clients in a way that displayed our sincerity in wanting to work with them.

What's more, we were politely relentless with prospects.

We positioned our firm's services so that potential clients could contact us when (not if) they were ready.

I recognized that we also made a point of arriving at meetings first to avoid keeping others waiting.

I realized that we abided by the follow-up philosophy of sending a thank-you to anyone who took more than 15 minutes to do something for us. (Yes, *anyone!*)

I realized that I loved what I did perhaps because I did what I loved (namely, telling people what to do—otherwise known as "giving advice"). As a result, I found it pretty easy to work 60-hour weeks.

One of our firm's policies was...and still is to schedule time to be "off duty" on weekends to spend time with family and friends. I realized how important this time was for reenergizing for the upcoming week.

I noticed that the quality of our services and our follow-through was so high that it "transformed" many of our clients into "marketing reps" by them recommending our services to *their* clients. My assistant and I always acknowledged (and still do) our raving fans with a little gift and a note within 24 hours of learning they had recommended us to another firm.

I consciously worked "on" business development during the most productive times of the day—and "in" the administration of the business before the workday began or after business hours. Any business practice we adopted three times became a *system* in our firm (for instance, documenting phone numbers when an organization was contacted more than once).

I realized that I did indeed have something to share with these savvy rainmakers. In fact, I had more information than I needed for a 45-minute talk.

The Sales Blitz event was a success and also the the starting point for a new workshop, "Key Ways for Accelerating Business Relationships."

Time passed. The more I presented this new workshop, the more convinced I became that relationship development was a foreign concept to many professionals. And how easy a problem to fix!

This book is offered as the solution to that problem. I hope the contents of *Courting Business* will assist you in seeing that relationship development is comprised of a system for getting others to develop a long-term relationship with you because of how you treat them. Its premise is that relationship development is the sum of the whole, the result of the habits that will become second nature for you when you put seemingly "little things" into practice that make a big difference in business.

This book has been written to be a quick read. It can be read in a few hours, or one message at a time. Each section describes a real-life situation, followed by "Courtship Tips" you can easily adapt into your professional routine.

What Does "Courting Business" Mean?

Courting business is the process of identifying your target market and getting prospects to want to do business with you.

Courting business is a highly structured activity with many well-known written and unwritten rules. Many individuals whose positions require them to generate revenue have never been exposed to what it takes to court business. Because of this lack of knowledge, they remain focused on their areas of expertise and dedicate less time to the relationship development process.

I often hear professionals who are responsible for maintaining business say, "Courting business is not my responsibility. I am on the receiving end—I step in after our salespeople close the business."

Wrong!

Whether your responsibility is reeling in the business or maintaining it, *Courting Business* is a must-read. This book will show you what it takes to attract clients and gives you the guidelines you need to keep those relationships strong.

COURTING

BUSINESS

How Is "Accelerating" Business Relationships Different From the Way You're Already Interacting With Prospects?

"Accelerating" business relationships means taking a proactive approach with both prospects and existing clients. It means keeping your name in front of them so they see that meeting their business needs is your priority.

Accelerating business relationships is different than the traditional way of doing business: it is systematic, whereas the traditional way of interacting with prospects and customers is sporadic.

The process of accelerating business relationships allows you to remain in control of business relationships. Instead of feeling rejected when prospects don't return your telephone calls or e-mail messages (which is a waste of time anyway), do you take some kind of constructive action?

Let me give you an example of how accelerating business works. Barbara, a retired banker, along with her husband, Ted, wanted to buy a condo in a community where only 30 units had been built. Each month they would drive through the neighborhood to see if one had been put on the market.

One day, Barbara got tired of waiting for one of the condos to go on the market and decided to take the situation into her own hands. She sent a letter to each of the 30 condo owners expressing the interest she and her husband had in their property. She invited each of them to call or e-mail her when they were ready to sell their condo.

Of course, timing is everything. It didn't happen *immediately*; however, within one year, Barbara and her husband heard from three of the condo owners who wanted to talk about selling their property to them. Guess where Barbara and Ted are living today? You got it: one of the addresses where their letter was sent.

The question is: *How can we apply the same principle to a variety of business opportunities?*

And here's another question that's just as important: *Why should we wait for opportunities to come to us when we can take action ourselves and accelerate them by being proactive?*

Courtship Tips
1. When you are serious about achieving a goal, find a creative way to achieve it.
2. You are more likely to acquire what you want by being proactive rather than reactive.

The Laws of Attraction

Birds do it instinctively. Bees do it naturally. And yet for some reason, people have to learn and relearn the "laws of attraction"—at least when it comes to putting the principles into action in a business setting!

The art of courting business is timeless. It requires mastering the laws of attraction relevant to the service or product you represent. No matter in what area of expertise you're interested, learning how to court business is essential for your success.

How Would You Rate Your Courtship Savvy?

Exercise

Rain, Rain Come My Way
Let New Business Make My Day!

Directions: Most people let business drizzle in rather than taking ownership of creating it. Take a few minutes to see how well you "make rain" (that is, generate revenue), and maybe even a little thunder!

1. What percentage of each day are you proactively selling rather than reactively acquiring business?

2. On average, how many "contacts" does it take to acquire a new client?

3. What percentage of the time do you send a follow-up letter in writing to prospects within 24 to 48 hours of making initial contact?

4. How many times during the last month have you asked prospects, "What is it going to take to earn your business?"

5. How many times a month do you keep your name in front of existing clients as a way of cross-selling?

6. When was the last time you made a conscientious effort to get on the same neurolinguistic wavelength as your prospects?

7. What courtship qualities do you have that make you unique?

It's Your Attitude, Not Your Aptitude, That Determines Your Altitude

In Zig Ziglar's book, *See You at the Top*, we read, "It's your attitude, not your aptitude, that determines your altitude." If ever there were a slogan worth pondering closely, it's that one!

Prospects equate your success with what they believe you can do for them. Your success is largely a function of your attitude and has little to do with how you ranked in your graduating class.

In fact, many academically successful people struggle in business when they are rejected by prospects several times before they get to a "yes." These academic superstars find the experience of rejection emotionally traumatic. They either learn to build a new attitude...or they get out of business.

Being politely persistent and determined eventually will pay off with prospects. By the same token, business "relationships" that emerge more or less instantly have a way of leaving (at least) one of the partners unhappy. What's the old saying? "If it looks too good to be true, it probably is."

Healthy business relationships take time to develop. Courtship is a critical part of that process. And attitude is a critical part of courtship.

Nothing important happens (at least as far as the relationship is concerned) until you establish meaningful rapport with your prospect.

Successful business courtship experts are "can-do" people. In other words, they delete negatives from their vocabulary. They tell their prospects what they can do rather than what they cannot do. They speak with confidence without being haughty.

Even the courtship experts who are Mensa members know that a high IQ or a postgraduate degree is simply not enough. They recognize that the knowledge about their service or product is secondary to the people skills they display with prospects and clients. Knowledge is important, however it can be even more valuable when you are able to first establish a one-on-one connection with prospects.

It is your attitude and emotional intelligence that support successful business relationships rather than merely having academic credentials or technical knowledge.

Courtship Tips

1. Emotional intelligence is what helps business relationships develop.

2. Demonstrating a mastery of the service you represent is important, however it must come after establishing rapport with your prospects.

The Power of Kevin Bacon's Six Degrees of Separation

When we opened our New York office, seven-day workweeks were common. One Sunday afternoon, after boarding a flight from New York to Cincinnati, I overheard the young man seated next to me talking on his cell phone with one of his college roommates. He was asking his roommate if he would pick him up from the airport. It appeared that his roommate's response was an emphatic "no." The football game on television took precedence over the 90-minute ride to the airport.

After the young man ended the conversation, he hung up and seemed to be deep in thought. He was trying to figure out how he was going to get from the airport to the university. After a few minutes, I asked him which university he attended, only to learn it was the same one from which my daughter had graduated!

As we got into a conversation, I mentioned that my home was in the same direction as the university and offered to get him to a halfway point—a spot where his roommate might reconsider the daunting task of picking him up. Luckily for my fellow passenger, his roommate did in fact reconsider his decision after learning that what had been a 90-minute trek was now only a 45-minute journey...and also included a promise of free pizza.

Now that the ride dilemma was solved, this young man and I continued talking. During the course of our conversation, I learned that he knew someone who knew a person who knew my daughter, who had graduated from the same university this young man attended. It all reminded me of the party game where you try to connect any given movie star in the history of motion pictures to a movie featuring the actor Kevin Bacon.

"What an amazing coincidence—talk about Kevin Bacon's Six Degrees of Separation," I exclaimed.

"That's really strange," replied the young man.

"Why do you say that?" I asked.

The young man replied, "My best friend's uncle *is* Kevin Bacon!"

Courtship Tips

1. Be proactive by helping people when they are in a pinch.

2. Remember that you are only six people away from the person about whom you have said, "I'd really like to meet so-and-so...."

The Power of a Compliment

Working with budding professionals is an education in itself. It is especially interesting to watch students in linear-thinking disciplines (for example, aspiring accountants, engineers, and architects) recognize what it takes to both land a job interview and, most importantly, outclass their competition and win the job.

One of the first rude awakenings of budding professionals is the realization that "there is no box" of active job leads waiting for you. They have to create their own box and fill it with leads! One of the most amazing stories I have heard to date about this principle was from a young man, whom I'll call Tom, who was a marketing major. He told me how he had landed a position with one of the biggest public relations firms in the country.

He was at a bookstore to find a book on "guerilla job hunting." On his way to the self-help section, he spotted a book written by the president of one of the firms where he could only dream of landing a job. After looking through it, he realized that it contained all the trials and tribulations that this CEO had encountered as he broke into the same industry Tom wanted to enter. Tom felt like he was reading about himself: he too was putting himself through school, and he also had overcome many personal obstacles in a mere 21 years.

Tom bought the book. He went home and read it cover to cover over a period of just two days. He was so inspired by this CEO for sharing his challenges and professional experience with readers that he dropped him a note of thanks. The correspondence conveyed how encouraging it was to young professionals to be reminded that everyone had to begin somewhere.

As it turned out, the CEO—a public relations guru—was quite flattered to receive Tom's note. He remembered beginning his own job search as he was preparing to graduate. What impressed the CEO the most was the initiative Tom had shown in composing and sending such a note. (Little did Tom know that the CEO made it a daily practice of writing three notes to existing clients and individuals...and encouraged his account executives to do the same.)

Tom had struck a definite nerve with his public relations idol. You can imagine how ecstatic he was to receive the follow-up correspondence from this CEO in his mailbox a week later. The CEO's note acknowledged receipt of his kind words. The best part about the note was the invitation to meet the CEO if his travels ever took him to the Big Apple.

Any marketing major or savvy job-hunting pro would have done exactly what this young man did. Tom phoned the CEO's assistant as directed to pass along a date when, as luck would have it, Tom would be in New York. The only open slot for the CEO that day was between noon and 1 p.m. The assistant scheduled a lunch get-together.

During the course of that lunch, the CEO was so impressed with Tom's professionalism and articulateness that he encouraged him to follow up with the firm's human resources manager. Can you guess who Tom works for today? And guess who footed the bill for the MBA degree he eventually pursued? You got it right: the CEO to whom he wrote a simple, personal note of thanks.

I hope this true story reinforces that a compliment can take you far.

Courtship Tips

1. Why waste kind thoughts! Make someone feel good by sharing them.

2. Write three notes a day to prospects and existing clients. It's a great way for you to let them know that they are in the forefront of your mind.

3. Recognize that your words have power.

4. The way you say something is as important as what you say.

Stroke, Don't Provoke

Many of us heard this advice from our mothers: *Either say something positive or avoid saying anything at all.*

Guess what? This same recommendation is a must-follow rule in business courtship.

When prospects talk about their competitors, other service providers, or even one of their colleagues in a negative light, you should avoid getting involved in the conversation. Instead, change the topic. If you must participate, share something positive.

The same applies when you are talking with someone who is grinding on your nerves.

No matter how difficult it is, listen to what your mom told you: *Stroke, don't provoke!*

Courtship Tip

1. You really do catch more flies with honey than with vinegar.

Follow the K.I.S.S. Rule

Courtship-friendly communication, whether it be verbal or written, is only as puzzling as you make it. It's all about boiling ideas down to their bare essentials.

You can have the best service or product since sliced bread; however, if you don't know how to position it in front of prospects in a way that makes them believe *they* found *you*, you may never earn their business!

Here's the point: If your letters, ad materials, and Website promotions aren't absolutely prospect-friendly and inviting, rewrite them! Offer all the technical details later, when your prospects ask about them.

When it comes to ad copy, write in short sentences. Combine the sentences into short paragraphs. Once you've made your point, stop writing!

Courtship Tip

1. Keep it simple.

Prospects Have to See Things Seven Times

If you have ever taken a marketing course, then you know that most prospects must see a message seven times to react to it. In my opinion, most people who attempt to be relationship developers fail for one reason: They believe that it's better to contact 20 prospects five times each rather than reaching out to 10 prospects 10 times each.

Successful rainmakers know that prospects are just warming up to them after five contacts. Just because prospects are slow to make decisions does not mean they are disinterested in establishing a working relationship. A prospect's deliberateness may simply mean that the timing is not yet right for the other person to establish a business relationship. It may mean that the bureaucracy is slowing down the process.

Most business relationships take an average of six months to a year to develop!

Check out how well you fare with developing business relationships by completing the following exercise:

 Exercise

Courting Your Prospects:
Most People Have to See Things
Seven Times to React

Take a few minutes to list the 10 top prospects you are presently "courting."

My Active Prospects	Check off the number of times you have had phone, in-person, or written contact with these prospects
1. _____	1 2 3 4 5 6 7
2. _____	1 2 3 4 5 6 7
3. _____	1 2 3 4 5 6 7
4. _____	1 2 3 4 5 6 7
5. _____	1 2 3 4 5 6 7
6. _____	1 2 3 4 5 6 7
7. _____	1 2 3 4 5 6 7
8. _____	1 2 3 4 5 6 7
9. _____	1 2 3 4 5 6 7
10. _____	1 2 3 4 5 6 7

> ### Courtship Tips
>
> 1. The average prospect must see things a minimum of seven times to react.
>
> 2. It's better to keep your name in front of 10 prospects 10 times rather than 20 prospects five times.
>
> 3. Most business relationships take an average of six months to a year to develop.

Court, Don't Call

The other day, a new associate asked me if I believe in developing prospects through telemarketing. My response to her was simple: *Court, don't call.*

It is so much more effective to get prospects to buy, rather than selling them your product or service. By positioning yourself with courtship strategies, prospects will believe they have found *you.*

> ### Courtship Tip
>
> 1. Get prospects to buy rather than selling to them.

Clients Are Prospects, Too!

It's an age-old sales and marketing rule:

80 percent of your business comes from
20 percent of your clients.

Are you focusing your primary efforts on the right 20 percent? Do you even know who the right 20 percent is? Here's an exercise that will help you put this principle into practice.

Exercise

Making the 80/20 Rule Work for You

Directions: Jot down your 20 top clients in the spaces below and identify the services you are presently providing to each client. Next, note the additional services from which these existing clients could benefit.

	Top Clients	Services Provided	Additional Services
1.			
2.			
3.			
4.			
5.			
6.			
7.			
8.			
9.			
10.			

	Top Clients	Services Provided	Additional Services
11.			
12.			
13.			
14.			
15.			
16.			
17.			
18.			
19.			
20.			

Creativity + Consistency = Courtship Success

Many rainmakers work hard. The ones who successfully court and convert prospects into clients recognize that acquiring them takes time. They also realize a principle I've already shared with you, namely that relationship development is a process rather than a single interaction.

Successful rainmakers also know that business decisions are made on PST (Prospect Standard Time) rather than the time frame in which *they* (the rainmakers) would like to close the business. They realize that having a positive attitude at all costs is crucial for sustaining a winning attitude.

Savvy rainmakers know that the courtship before business is acquired can sometimes take a year or longer. They keep their names in front of prospects monthly as a means of staying on people's minds.

Those who successfully close the courtship circle execute the process by having a strategic plan for developing this working relationship. This plan includes creative tools for making the prospect connection.

One of the most successful tools that I have found works is a "Tip of the Month" postcard. This four-color, oversize postcard marketing tool has been a simple way for our firm to stay in the forefront of the minds of prospects and clients. As you will see in the following example, a Tip of the Month format educates prospects and existing clients about the services you represent in an educational and informative way. Whether they read it, share it, or toss it, your organization still remains in the subconscious of prospects and clients. They will remember you when they are ready to invest time, energy, and dollars in securing the service or product you represent.

A Tip of the Month postcard accelerates the courtship process. It keeps your name in front of people 12 times a year. Imagine the impact! If you already send a quarterly newsletter, consider augmenting it with a monthly postcard. Imagine what three times the exposure—at minimal cost—could do for your business.

Dear Professional:

Happy New Year! I hope 2004 is off to a great start for you.

As you may know, At Ease Inc. is beginning its 18th year. My staff and I hope you will accept a monthly *gift of knowledge* from us. This month's etiquette tip focuses on why your choice of words is so important. I hope you both enjoy and benefit from it.

Sincerely,

Ann Marie Sabath, Founder - At Ease Inc.
Author, *Business Etiquette: 101 Ways To Conduct Business With Charm & Savvy*
Author, *Beyond Business Casual: What To Wear To Work If You Want To Get Ahead*
Author, *The International Etiquette Book Series*

JANUARY 2004 TIP OF THE MONTH
HOW TO AVOID SOUND BARRIERS WHEN TALKING WITH OTHERS

The way you communicate your thoughts is as important as the message itself. One term that can unknowingly act as a sound barrier is the word, "but." During a recent workshop, I asked participants why "but" should be deleted from their vocabulary. One individual said, "When *but* is used in a sentence, an excuse usually follows it."

The next time you are ready to use "but," try substituting it with the term "however." You may be pleasantly surprised to find that people listening to you will hear the word "however" as a transitional term rather than the sound barrier that "but" may create.

Here's a quick review of your upcoming tips of the month:

February	*Raising Your People Awareness Through The Rule Of Three*
March	*The Secret To Adding Presence To Business Casual Attire*
April	*Table Talk: Your Responsibility During Business Meals*
May	*Why Being On Time Is Considered Late To Many*
June	*An Important Courtesy To Extend When Using Your Cell Phone*
July	*Why Counting To Two Is So Important*
August	*The Value Of Asking Clients For A Specific Amount Of Time*
September	*How To Let A Server Know You Are Hosting A Meal*
October	*The Way To Add Warmth To E-Mail Messages*
November	*Getting People To Say Yes Through The Rule Of Seven*
December	*Business Card Etiquette*

Do You Have A Business Etiquette Question?
Call us at 800-873-9909 or e-mail it to us at etiquette@ateaseinc.com

AT·EASE·INC·
BUSINESS PROTOCOL & ETIQUETTE

www.corporateetiquette.com • www.universityetiquette.com

*Give The Individuals In Your Organization That Edge
By Integrating Our Programs Into Your Upcoming Meeting!*

©2004 At Ease Inc.

Many clients ask if sending the Tip of the Month via e-mail would be as effective as one via "snail mail." Although a mass e-mail certainly would be less costly in terms of time and money, I consider it to be less effective. Why? Because the idea is to stand out, and the quickest way to get lost in the crowd is to send an e-mail.

When you want to stand out, market against the waves. In other words, do what the majority of people avoid—use snail mail. And if you'd like to increase your odds of getting your Tip of the Month postcard noticed even more, try dropping your mailing on a Saturday. The reason? There's a good chance your postcard will be received on Tuesday, which is the lightest day for mail (except for holiday weeks). If it is a holiday week, wait until the following Saturday to drop your mailing.

First class or bulk? That's easy: first class! While bulk mailings are fine for catalog mailings, a good old-fashioned first-class postage stamp affixed to your organization's Tip of the Month postcard shows that a real live human being took time to affix it. As slight as that human touch may seem to be in this case, it certainly is warmer than meter postage or a bulk mailing designation. People really do notice these touches!

The most challenging part of the Tip of the Month postcard is taking time to write copy. My suggestion: Reserve one full day over the weekend to write out all 12 postcards. By doing so, you will be set for the year. Imagine how good you will feel to have accomplished this goal!

Once you begin the mailings, maintain credibility with your prospects and clients by consistently having them sent on the first Saturday of each month. A surefire way to avoid letting other projects keep you from sending your tips is by both preparing and printing them in December for the following year, then mailing them once a month as outlined in this chapter.

Courtship Tips

1. Stay encouraged by remembering that courting business is a process.

2. Create a strategic plan for keeping your name in front of prospects and existing clients.

3. Stay in touch, literally, by mailing a monthly Tip of the Month or other form of written communication to prospects—*every* month.

4. Position your mailing so that it is delivered on Tuesday, the lightest day for receiving mail.

5. Commit to this monthly mailing by preparing the text and then printing the postcards one year in advance. Once you've done that, you will definitely send the darned things out!

What are you doing to keep your name in front of prospects? If you would like a set of 12 "Tips of the Month" developed for your organization's marketing purposes, contact At Ease Inc., at (800) 873-9909 or courtshiptips@ateaseinc.com.

Keep Your Prospects "Warm"

Successful rainmakers are the first to recognize that there are only so many hours in the day, so many days in the week, so many weeks in a month, and so many months in a year. Successful dealmakers look at the big picture. Although they focus their attention on hot prospects, they recognize the importance of their mid-level prospects (who may have a need for their service within, say, the next two years) and their low-level prospects (who may not have a need for their service for the next several years). The job is to keep these "cold" prospects "warm."

While you are actively courting hot prospects, use the ideas in this book to remain in the forefront of the minds of your cold prospects. By doing so, you may see the business seeds you've planted with them begin to sprout in the future. You've already invested some of your valuable time with them. Keep the relationship alive through an occasional e-mail, with a Tip of the Month mailing, or by means of other marketing tools designed by your organization. Also, make

sure to keep track of your relationship with prospects. (See the following sample ledger entries.)

4-28-04	**Investigative Firm** 614-555-1212 Alan Kline
	655 Monarch, Columbus, OH 43365
	akline@hsminvestigative.com
	Alan contacted our firm after reading the article in *Inc.*
	E-mailed a proposal to Alan about "10 Key Ways for Gaining
	That Competitive Edge."
	Offered June 15, June 30, July 26, or July 28.
	Added the owner of the company to the corporate excel list to receive
	the Tip of the Month
	Mailed the information packet and a copy of the blue 101 ways to Alan to
	share with the owner
	Marked the calendar to follow up on May 5, when the proposal is due.
5-4-04	Spoke with Alan. The owner is reviewing the information packet and book.
	E-mailed Alan to let him know that we look forward to working with him when
	the time is right.
5-26-04	Left a voice mail for Alan to learn what it will take to earn their business.
6-28-04	E-mailed Alan to learn if they would like to secure July 26 or July 28.
6-30-04	Alan e-mailed us to let us know they do not have the funding at this time.
	Sent a follow-up e-mail to Alan to let him know we look forward to working with
	his team when the time is right.

Cold Prospect

6-22-04	**XYZ Law Firm** 312-555-1212 Nancy Bernard

6-22-04   **XYZ Law Firm**   312-555-1212   Nancy Bernard
123 Any Street, Chicago, IL 60606
nbernard@xyz.com
Nancy contacted us about working with their First Years, Summers, and perhaps Partners.
E-mailed Nancy a proposal for working together.
Sent Nancy the client contact sheet, along with a few evaluation summaries.
Added Nancy to the Tip of the Month list.
Quoted a specific amount for a 60- or 90-minute program.

7-22-04   E-mailed Nancy to learn how she would like to proceed.

9-10-04   E-mailed Nancy to let her know that we will be working with another client in Chicago on October 7.
Is she interested in securing a program?
Nancy e-mailed back to confirm she would like to observe the October 7 program.
Nancy shared the name of another individual at the firm who would like to observe the session. (Carol)
Marked calendar to contact Nancy on September 13 to confirm the location for October 7.
Added Carol to the Tip of the Month list.

9-13-04   E-mailed the program specifics to Nancy for the October 7 session. She will share them with Carol.

10-4-04   E-mailed our contact for the October 7 program to share that Nancy and Carol would like to observe the session on Thursday.

10-8-04   Sent a follow-up thank-you to Nancy and Carol for taking time from their busy schedules to observe the October 7 session.

11-9-04   E-mailed Nancy to let her know that January 19 and 20 are available for her team.
E-mailed Carol to let her know that January 19 and 20 are currently available.

11-11-04   Followed up with Carol and offered May 24 & 25; and June 1, 7 & 8 for their Summer Associates
Quoted a certain amount because we will be working in Chicago at that time

12-6-04   Followed-up with Carol to let her know that another client has secured May 25.
Is there a particular date she would like us to secure for their team?

Warm Prospect

Courtship Tip

1. Keep both warm and cold prospects "warm" by keeping your name in front of them on a regular basis.

If You're on Time, You're Late!

Who do you know who likes to be kept waiting?

Organized people make a point of getting to places early. Disorganized people are notorious for showing up to meetings late.

Savvy professionals know that it is always better to arrive at meetings early than to be labeled as the one who keeps others waiting. People who show up a few minutes early for a meeting look prepared. When you're early, you also project the high value that you place on others' time. Individuals who make a point of getting to meetings just a few minutes early also know that the first person there subconsciously has the upper hand. Think about it. The individual who shows up last for meetings frequently feels vulnerable for sliding into home base late. My experience is that this person is frequently called "out"! Have you ever noticed that the person who shows up late for a meeting starts off at a disadvantage and may feel obliged to give in to the recommendations of others?

People who arrive late are unknowingly handing business to their competition. Prospects often believe that people who cannot manage their time probably cannot manage their money well either, or perhaps even the project being discussed!

Make a point of getting to your out-of-office meetings a few minutes early. Besides being labeled as professional, you also will be demonstrating your mastery of an important business courtship rule.

Courtship Tip

1. Let your prospects see how much you've been looking forward to meeting with them by arriving a few minutes early.

Write Down the Time You Have to Leave Rather Than the Time You Have to Be Somewhere

If you've already created the habit of controlling your schedule, you know that promptness pays big dividends.

I was born two weeks late, and for most of my life I seemed to have a knack for sliding into meetings just on time and sometimes even after the fact for the first 10 years of my career. I would blame it on traffic, the accident on the freeway, or the family/career balancing act.

One day I finally woke up thanks to an investment advisor my husband thought walked on water. I remember my spouse and I sitting at a restaurant waiting for this person, who was notorious for being late. After 15 minutes I said to my husband—who had the patience of Job—"Honey, I will make a second vow to you that from this day forward I will always write down the time we have to leave rather than the time we have to be somewhere. I see how incredibly unprofessional it is to keep others waiting."

My husband, who was known to be consistently early, couldn't believe his ears. It had been a bone of contention between us for years. "In exchange," I continued, "I have one request for you. Let's find another investment counselor. After all, if this person can't manage his time, how in the world can he manage our money?"

Luckily, my husband saw the correlation between time and money and acknowledged his willingness to look into other financial advisors.

Fifteen minutes later, our soon-to-be-former investment counselor arrived. He apologized profusely for being late, using the excuse that his last client took longer than he expected.

What message did that send to us about how important we were to him?

That was our last meeting with him. I remember thinking to myself, *You learn two things from everyone: what to do and what not to do.*

It was also the beginning of the new me—the person who began writing down the time I had to leave rather than the time I had to be somewhere. I still do it. You should, too.

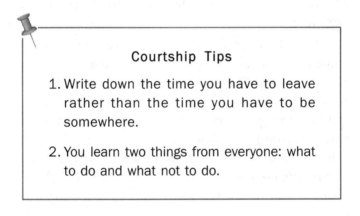

Courtship Tips

1. Write down the time you have to leave rather than the time you have to be somewhere.

2. You learn two things from everyone: what to do and what not to do.

People Tend to Be More Willing to Give You Their Time When You Ask for a Specific Amount of It

I'll always remember my first phone encounter with Jean LaPointe, who was the manager of organizational development with Chiquita Brands. He called our office to schedule a meeting to discuss developing a training relationship between our firm and his organization. Even though he was the prospect, he made me feel as though I was doing him a favor by asking, "When can you spare 30 minutes from your busy schedule to meet with me?"

What class! And how easy it was for me to say "yes!"

We scheduled the meeting for a mutually convenient date and time. I sent a follow-up letter to Mr. LaPointe with background information about our firm.

Our meeting day arrived. After being welcomed into his office and being offered a seat, Jean LaPointe said, "Thank you for taking time to meet with me for a half hour." He explained his specific training interest and asked how our firm could accomplish this goal. During the last 10 minutes of our meeting, Jean said, "Ann Marie, during the next few minutes, what else may I share with you in order for you to prepare a proposal for me?"

That 30-minute meeting was the beginning of our firm's training relationship with this world-class operation. It also was the way I learned to get prospects to see me by asking for a specific amount of their time.

Courtship Tips

1. When scheduling meetings, ask individuals for a specific amount of time.

2. Send a follow-up note confirming your prearranged meeting.

3. At the beginning of the meeting, thank the person for meeting with you for the mutually agreed upon period of time.

Help Your Prospects With Your Homework: Get Your Competitors on the Table

Sound the alarm! The prospect wants to meet with you to discuss the possibility of doing business together. Before going to the appointment, do your homework. Learn about what your competition is offering.

During the course of the meeting, ask your prospect if they have had a chance to visit with some of your competitors. They may be surprised by this question. Continue by sharing one or two attributes about your competition; for instance, "ABC Company has been in business 35 years.

Since you met with them, you have probably seen that this group is comprised of very competent professionals."

Then, in the very next breath, sell the benefits of what your organization has to offer your prospect over your competition; for instance, say:

"Our business is 20 years old, with a team of professionals that cumulatively offers 50 years of experience to you. In addition, you will always have two contacts. We stagger our schedules so that if one of us is with another client or on vacation, your needs will still be met promptly.

"Finally, we recognize that promptness pays. Our organization's motto is that all calls are to be returned by the end of each work day. Our clients tell us that our responsive manner alone is enough reason for earning their business. I hope you will see this, as we do, as an important benefit."

Courtship Tips

1. Know the competition and make brief positive comments about them. Doing so builds your own credibility and expertise, and it makes you look more appealing.

2. Immediately sell the benefit of what you have to offer.

Court Your Prospects by Finding
Common Ground With Them

Two years after launching our business, we landed a nonprofit client. Because this client had 32 other counterparts across the country with new members annually, we soon realized that in time this nonprofit business could become a division in itself for our firm.

After giving the matter a good deal of thought, my staff and I realized that it would be better to court the top 10 offices rather than the 22 smaller ones with fewer members. Within two years, the offices in Washington, D.C.; Houston; Dallas; Richmond; Columbus; Louisville; Cleveland; Cincinnati; and Raleigh signed on with our firm. Detroit was next. Since this last city housed the third-largest nonprofit that we were targeting, I knew that we had to do whatever was necessary to acquire it.

I sent a letter of introduction in January to the appropriate person, Charlene. One week later I placed a follow-up call.

The good news: Charlene accepted my call. The bad news: Their vendor/bidding cycle was in November for the following membership year rather than February, as it was in the other offices. I asked whether I could contact her the following August to discuss having our proposal considered for the following membership year. I had the impression that her "yes" was offered only to get me off the phone.

As soon as I hung up, a letter was sent to Charlene thanking her for her time and letting her know that I would indeed be contacting her in six months to begin our discussions for working together.

During the second week of August, I called Charlene and reached her on the first try. I let her know that I was going to be in Detroit in three weeks and asked if we could meet. She explained that the timing was bad because she would be in the midst of their membership drive. I asked if we could schedule an early breakfast or quick lunch. Her response: "Out of the question."

"How about dinner?" I pushed.

"Impossible," she said. "I'm a single mother and need to be with my daughter after work."

"I'm a single mom, too," I shared. "How about if the three of us go to dinner? Your daughter can choose the restaurant of her choice. I would really like to meet with you, Charlene."

There was a pause...and then Charlene conceded that dinner might work.

Once again, I sent a thank-you letter solidifying the agreed-upon date and time later that month. When the day arrived, I showed up at Charlene's office and went with her to pick up her daughter. We then headed to the restaurant of her daughter's choice. When we arrived at Chuck E. Cheese's (what we do to earn business!), we ordered her daughter's favorite pizza and then sent her off to the playroom with coins in hand to play games until the meal arrived.

Charlene said to me, "Ann Marie, I must admit that the only reason I'm sitting here with you this evening is because of your impressive follow-up. I was shocked when you called me six months after we had first spoken. I recognize that you really want to work with our members."

That evening was the beginning of a 10-year business relationship that has been both enjoyable and lucrative. It took courtship strategies that I didn't know I possessed at the time. Yet they were all rooted in an idea I *did* know a lot about: *finding common ground with your prospects.*

This courtship business experience proved what it took to earn a new account. If it came down to it again, I would even eat another meal at Chuck E. Cheese's...if that would be what it would take to appease my prospect's family.

Courtship Tips

1. It takes the same amount of energy to do business with the little fish as it does with the big fish. Think big!

2. Before contacting a new prospect by phone, first send a letter of introduction.

3. Get prospects to say "yes" at the end of conversations.

4. Follow up in writing with prospects and clients after speaking with them by phone or meeting with them in person.

5. Do what you say and say what you do. People are impressed with individuals who keep their word.

6. Be politely relentless.

7. Find a shared interest that can act as the launching pad for your new business relationship.

Making the Connection Through the Likeability Factor

Learning how to be likeable is an important success skill. Business really is built more on relationships rather than on the service or product represented.

Although you may have the best product or service to offer, that alone is only part of the relationship development equation. What prospects want is a connection—the kind of connection that will make doing business with you a pleasant experience.

There are many ways this principle plays out. The simplest is probably familiar to you already: asking about the family photo the person has prominently placed in the office. Courting prospects also may include beginning your face-to-face encounter, e-mail message, or telephone call by asking about the recent trip the person said he or she was going to take the last time you spoke.

Prospects see us as *interesting* when we are sincerely—I repeat, *sincerely!*—*interested* in them.

Guess what? Prospects are actually willing to invest more when they enjoy the company of vendors. They find it painful to do business with individuals who are so infatuated with their own expertise that they don't bother to ask others about what's happening in their world.

People who have mastered the likeability factor know that a meeting with a prospect has been successful when they have learned more about the other person than they have shared about themselves.

Try the following the next time you are with prospects:

- ◆ Ask questions about the other person(s).
- ◆ Only offer information about yourself when asked.
- ◆ Answer questions directed to you in a succinct fashion, following your answer by asking another question of the person(s) in your midst.
- ◆ Notice the people who monopolize the conversation by focusing on their own expertise.
- ◆ Recognize the people who found what you had to say as being more interesting than their own words of wisdom.
- ◆ Ask yourself who you consider to be the most likeable person in the group. (More often than not, you will choose the person who focused more on you rather than on his or her own world.)

Courtship Tips

1. Savvy rainmakers learn to be likeable by asking others about themselves.

2. People see you as *interesting* when you are *interested* in what they have to say.

3. The power of listening usually trumps the power of speech.

◆ *Enhancing Your Telephone Presence* ◆

Shape your telephone image through your word choice. By doing so, others will respect, like, and want to work with you.

Negative Terms	vs.	Positive Terms
"I'll have to check…"		"I'll be glad to check for you."
"I'd hate to…"		"I want to…"
"May I ask your name?"		"What is your name please?"
"Can I interrupt for a minute?"		"May we talk briefly?"
"Can you spell your name for me?"		"Please spell that for me."
"If I can find out…"		"When I confirm…"
"I'm only the…"		"I'm the receptionist and will be glad to connect you with…"

◆ ◆ ◆

Be Friendly to Everyone—
Even on the Subway!

Some people have never met a stranger. I'm one of them.

Four years after we opened our New York office, I decided to take my first subway ride alone. I was highly motivated. I was going to Chinatown!

I got on the subway and, as soon as a seat became available, sat down next to a young man in his mid-20s. Even though I knew where I was going, I wanted to talk to someone, so I said to this person, "Excuse me. Will this train get me to Chinatown?"

He acknowledged that it would and then asked from where I was visiting. We talked for about 15 minutes, and then I pulled out the business card that just happened to be in my pocket, extended my hand, and said, "Thank you for making my first subway ride so pleasant. I'm Ann Marie Sabath."

As we shook hands, he said, "It's been nice talking with you, Ann Marie. I'm Todd Jenkins."

I continued with, "Todd, if you drop me an e-mail, I'd love to send you a copy of one of my books."

Todd leaned down, and out of his computer bag came a business card. We soon bid our farewells and off we went.

As soon as I got off the train, I had this strange feeling that I really should send Todd the thank-you note and book I had promised him as soon as possible. I called my office, and thanks to my hyper-efficient assistant, the note and book were on their way to Todd that afternoon.

Guess what? For four years I stayed in touch with Todd through quarterly e-mail notes acknowledging the good press his organization received, and holiday greetings. And then four years and one month after our meeting on the subway, Todd called our office.

My assistant buzzed me: "There's a Todd Jenkins on the line."

"My subway man?" I asked.

My assistant responded, "What?"

"Never mind," I replied. "Please put him through."

I answered the line with, "Good afternoon, Todd. This is Ann Marie. It's so good hearing from you."

He replied, "Thank you for taking my call. Do you remember me?"

I said, "You bet I do."

He continued, "Ann Marie, I'm on a committee at our firm that is looking for client relationship training. Would you be interested in meeting with our committee so we can see what you have to offer?"

That one was pretty easy to answer. "Name the date and time, Todd," I said, "and I'll be there."

That subway ride and conversation four years later became the catalyst for a big chunk of business for my company.

The moral: *Being friendly pays big dividends.*

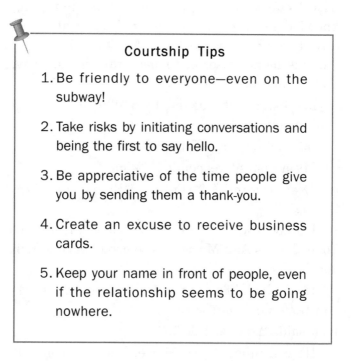

Courtship Tips

1. Be friendly to everyone—even on the subway!

2. Take risks by initiating conversations and being the first to say hello.

3. Be appreciative of the time people give you by sending them a thank-you.

4. Create an excuse to receive business cards.

5. Keep your name in front of people, even if the relationship seems to be going nowhere.

Putting the Platinum Rule Into Practice

Whereas average professionals put the Golden Rule into practice, the most savvy professionals live by the "Platinum Rule." Rather than merely doing to others as they would have done to them, the most seasoned professionals go above and beyond for everyone. Instead of doing what others expect of them, they do whatever is necessary to exceed expectations.

Similarly, they involve themselves in philanthropic activities for the sake of the cause rather than to find out what they can get out of it.

These stellar individuals walk their talk and make a habit of being nice to everyone. They are proactively nice. They initiate eye contact and greetings with others, and they jot personal notes to prospects and community members when they receive good press or when they reach major life events in their family, such as births, marriages, or deaths.

Individuals who have mastered this Platinum Rule also practice the "Rule of Three." In other words, whenever they are within 3 feet of someone and appear to have an interest in common, they initiate a conversation.

Savvy rainmakers also are risk-takers—if you call initiating conversation a risk. They do it so often that it becomes the norm for them.

So, do you live by the Golden Rule or by the Platinum Rule? How often do you make a point of acknowledging individuals in your organization who are entering the building or waiting in the lobby of your organization? How often do you write notes to celebrate a contact's triumph or to offer condolences during hard times? How often do you follow the Rule of Three?

Courtship Tips

1. Go above and beyond for everyone. When you make being nice a habit, it becomes second nature...and it doesn't feel like work.

2. Make a point of initiating eye contact with others first. The same goes for greetings.

3. Acknowledge others whenever they are within 3 feet of you. It's amazing how far a smile or nod can take you!

You Don't Have to Be Bilingual to Speak Your Prospect's Language

In a recent training program, we discussed the importance of finding a common denominator with prospects. We also discussed how easy it was to establish common ground with individuals from abroad.

One of our Seattle workshop participants mentioned that she went to Bali for business. Each time she rode in a taxi, she asked the drivers how to pronounce a particular phrase she found in her Balinese language guide. Before long, she became comfortable with simple phrases such as "good morning," "good afternoon," "please," and "thank you." This person did more than learn a few words in another language—she also ignited smiles on the faces of many people throughout her trip. The effort she was making to speak a few words in Balinese went a very long way.

I gave a similar example of requesting an omelette at a casual breakfast buffet. When I was told that only over-easy and scrambled eggs were available, I said that either would be fine. I also noticed that the chef was Hispanic, and I asked, "De dónde es?" (From where are you?)

He responded, "Soy de Guatemala—y usted?"

Before long, he was smiling broadly and asking me in Spanish what I wanted on my omelette!

It's amazing what a few words in your prospect's native tongue can do to establish a rapport that otherwise might not exist. As you see, it can make what could have been a mediocre situation quite a pleasant one.

Courtship Tip

1. Make an effort to become acquainted with the language and cultural nuances of those around you. It just may help you to advance a relationship.

Prospects Don't Care How Much You Know Until They Know How Much You Care

For two consecutive years, I had a contract for 24 pieces of business with one of the Big Four accounting firms.

At the end of the second year I got some good news: the training had been very well received by all the participants. I also learned that the person with whom I had a long-standing relationship had been promoted and the position had been filled by someone else, which meant I would have a new contact.

Anyone who has ever been in this situation knows what this means: the courtship process was about to begin again. My goal was to gain the confidence of this new prospect, whose name was Julie, so that she would integrate 12 additional training programs into the company's upcoming curriculum. As a way of jump-starting the relationship, I asked Julie's predecessor to send a letter of reference to her about how well our training was received. For two consecutive months, I tried to make contact with Julie—to no avail.

The new responsibility she had undertaken was in addition to her existing projects, so that told me that her interest in developing a working relationship with me appeared to be low on her list of priorities.

One day I decided to call Julie to try to find out how close she was to making a curriculum decision. Once again, my call went to her voice mail. Rather than leaving a message that I felt certain would be ignored—just as my past messages had—I decided to see if Julie's assistant could tell me when she would be available to take my call. When her assistant shared that Julie would not be in that week, I casually asked whether she was on vacation.

"No," her assistant said. "Julie's mom is having surgery, so she went home to be with her. If all goes well, she will return to the office next week."

"Thank you for letting me know," I said. "I'll call Julie in a few weeks."

Little did I know that what came naturally to me in this situation was what was going to take this business relationship to the next level.

Because I was very close to my own mother, I could easily imagine the worry that Julie was experiencing. I dropped Julie a note to let her know that I had learned about her mother's surgery from her assistant. I shared that my thoughts and prayers were with her and her mother.

Two weeks later I placed another call to Julie. This time she picked up the phone. Did she answer the line because I had caught her at a good time...or was it because she recognized my number? I'll never know. What I do know, however, is that she was very pleased to hear from me.

The first question I asked her was how her mother was doing. There was good news: surgery had been successful. Near the end of the conversation I also learned that Julie had decided to integrate our program into the company's national curriculum for the third consecutive year.

Twelve more pieces of business—and further confirmation of the time-tested principle that people don't care how much you know until they know how much you care.

Courtship Tips

1. Make your prospects your raving fans by getting them to send letters of endorsement to key contacts.

2. When prospects aren't responsive, take it professionally rather than personally.

3. Be proactive by learning about your prospects from those around them.

4. When your prospects are experiencing personal trauma, let them know you care.

5. Follow up.

Kerchoo! Keep Cold Calls From Creating a Chilling Effect With Prospects

Cold calls can cause shivers up many prospects' spines. Many organizations sabotage their reputations by contracting with outside companies to "generate leads" through either live or computer-generated telemarketing strategies.

Rather than taking the risk of turning off potential clients through cold calls, I suggest that you warm up your prospects by finding a common interest. You can sometimes do this by perusing their Websites to learn what is "new" in their organization. You can also play off recent press the person has received. Another good way to preheat a cold call is to find someone who knows your prospect and is willing to precede your call with an e-mail message or personal introduction to that prospect.

If your organization requires that you make cold calls as a lead-generating technique, be as cordial with prospects when they tell you they are *not* interested in the service you represent as you are with those who want to know more. Whatever you do, avoid hanging up on disinterested prospects without first thanking the person for the few minutes you had to speak together. Recognize that you are in the role of ambassador for your organization even with prospects who are *not* interested in your service or product.

If you want prospects to see you as sincere in establishing a relationship with them, try sending a thank-you note for the few minutes they *did* spend talking with you. You will be surprised how a "no" today can turn into a "yes" tomorrow...and how often a cold call eventually turns into a hot prospect.

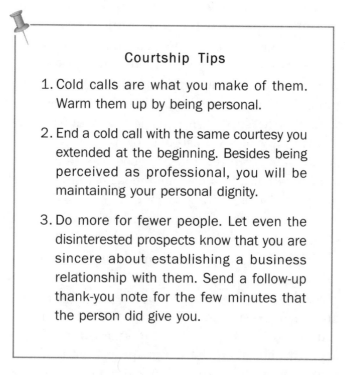

Courtship Tips

1. Cold calls are what you make of them. Warm them up by being personal.

2. End a cold call with the same courtesy you extended at the beginning. Besides being perceived as professional, you will be maintaining your personal dignity.

3. Do more for fewer people. Let even the disinterested prospects know that you are sincere about establishing a business relationship with them. Send a follow-up thank-you note for the few minutes that the person did give you.

The Secret for Getting Your Ideas Accepted

This is one example of form being as important than substance. You will get your ideas accepted to the degree that they appear (plausibly) to arise from subjects your contacts have raised in previous conversations.

Prospects and clients want to do business with individuals who know how to listen—a core value in relationship development. One way to demonstrate your excellent listening skills is to frame what you have to share against something your prospect or new client already told you (for instance, "During our last meeting, you mentioned..." or "Based on your comments...").

By building your conversation on these "connectors," you will find yourself talking to more attentive prospects and clients. Remember, people will see you as more interesting when you demonstrate your interest in what they have said to you.

Many people ask, "How in the world can you remember details about individuals to use as 'connectors'?" The answer is really very simple: by jotting down notes about the individual following your conversation!

Some people try to contact too many prospects. Successful rainmakers, however, contact *fewer* prospects, remembering *more* about each one.

They keep their business door open by documenting what they learned from their prospects after
every meeting. They realize that this data is important for future encounters.

Courtship Tips

1. Recognize that form is as important as
   substance.

2. Integrate conversation connectors into
   your professional style.

Always Leave Them Wanting More

Ultimately, I think courting prospects is a
matter of psychology. When prospects enjoy your
company and respect your expertise, you will find
that you are naturally on track for developing a
long-term relationship with them. The trick is
getting them to enjoy your company and respect
your expertise.

One way to be sure you are creating a pleasant experience is to avoid overextending your
stay. In fact, many successful rainmakers I know
make a point of cutting off meetings a few minutes earlier than the allotted time they have
scheduled.

When possible, try to end your meetings on a high note. Stress the positive; emphasize what *can* happen next. By doing this, you will create a pleasant experience and leave your prospects wanting more.

Courtship Tips

1. Recognize that courting business is a matter of psychology.

2. Try ending meetings a few minutes earlier that the time allotted. You will be demonstrating good time-management skills and also a respect for your prospects' time.

3. End your meetings on a high note.

If You Don't Have Time to Do It Right the First Time, What Makes You Believe You'll Have Time Later?

Procrastination means putting off doing something. The only thing worse than procrastination is not doing it at all!

We've all done it. You've meant to send that thank-you note, that congratulatory letter, or even that sympathy card. You were so busy you put it off until later that day. Yet time got away from you.

You jotted yourself a note to do it later in the week. It was one of those hectic weeks, so you put off that follow-up note until the weekend.

You forgot to take home your business note cards and promised yourself that you'll do it first thing Monday morning. Your boss stops by your office and the morning gets away from you. You promise yourself you'll take the note card and envelope home that evening.

One week passes from the time the note should have gone out. You're wondering if it's too late. Perhaps it would be better not to send it at all, considering that it's been so long. You decide not to send the note.

The scenario just described is common. However, who wants to be a common person? People who successfully court business want to stand out and exceed the expectations of their prospects and clients.

What is it that you've been putting off, promising yourself you will take the time to do it by the end of the workday? Whatever it is, identify it.

Do it now.

Do it right.

Courtship Tips

1. Do it now.

2. Do it right the first time.

Use a System to Navigate Your Day

How well do you use your workday minutes?

Successful professionals have a daily system for mapping out their relationship development schedule. They know what to do to develop prospect relationships and ultimately convert those relationships to clients. They schedule more time to work "on" business than they do "in" business.

Most professionals who successfully court prospects have a methodology that they follow. They make a point of working "on" business at least 60 percent of the week. They schedule the remaining time for working "in" business.

In order to effectively manage their time, they schedule their daily "on" business activities during the most productive hours of the day (for example, 9 a.m. to 4 p.m.). The 7 a.m. to 9 a.m. and 4 p.m. to 6 p.m. hours are then reserved for working on "in" business activities.

"On" business activities include keeping your name in front of prospects in one or more of the following ways:

- Visiting with prospects by phone or e-mail.
- Scheduling meetings with prospects.
- Networking during business/social gatherings.
- Sending a follow-up thank-you whenever it takes someone more

than 15 minutes to do something for you.

◆ Mailing that copy of "good ink" to a prospect or client acknowledged in the news.

"In" business activities include one or more of the following:

◆ Doing administrative tasks.

◆ Preparing your weekly report.

◆ Reorganizing your files.

◆ Preparing a speech that you've been asked to deliver.

You can be certain that by focusing on both types of business activities and allotting the appropriate amount of time for each, you will successfully court your prospects. In turn, a high percentage of them will turn into clients because of the time and energy you expended.

Courtship Tips

1. Map out your relationship development schedule on a daily basis.

2. Get the most out of each day by focusing on "on" business activities for at least 60 percent of the day, reserving the rest of your time for "in" business activities.

Analyze Your Business Day

Exercise

Do You Spend the Majority of Your Day Working "on" Business or "in" Business?

Directions: Take a few minutes to log what you accomplished during your last business day. Next to each action, note whether the business activity was "on" business or "in" business.

(Remember: "On" business means developing or maintaining a prospect relationship by getting on base or scoring a run. "In" business means doing administrative work, participating in meetings, or making calls unrelated to prospect development.)

	"On" Business	"In" Business
7 a.m.	_____	_____
8 a.m.	_____	_____
9 a.m.	_____	_____
10 a.m.	_____	_____
11 a.m.	_____	_____
Noon	_____	_____

(Continued...)

	"On" Business	"In" Business
1 p.m.	_____	_____
2 p.m.	_____	_____
3 p.m.	_____	_____
4 p.m.	_____	_____
5 p.m.	_____	_____
Evening	_____	_____

If more than 40 percent of your day was involved with "in" business activities rather than "on" business activities, you should either delegate your "in" business activities or work on them before the workday officially begins or after it ends.

Anything You Have Done More Than Three Times in Exactly the Same Way Should Be Empowered to One of Your Team Members

This is a critical rule for success! A savvy rainmaker remains the frontline person for prospects and delegates the behind-the-scenes administrative work to one of his team members.

When a rainmaker does not have someone to whom work can be delegated, that person must concentrate on "in" business tasks before the day begins or after work hours. A rainmaker realizes that the way to be productive is to create as much time as possible to network by focusing "on" creating opportunities—working, in other words, to keep his face, voice, and correspondence in front of prospects.

A productive rainmaker creates a system that can be easily taught to the person(s) he empowers to work on administrative tasks. He teaches the system then reviews the work the first few times. If the person who was delegated the work completed the task correctly, the person is complimented. If the person does the task wrong, the rainmaker reviews the system with the person for a second time and then asks the person to correct the error.

An effective rainmaker does not spend his time micromanaging. Instead, the person builds a team who can keep existing client relationships active as he develops new ones.

If you've done something the exact same way three times, you should build a system, teach it to someone else, and hold that person accountable for the results!

Courtship Tips

1. Learn the power of delegating.

2. Anything you do the exact same way three times in a row should be delegated to a team member.

Work as Though Your Salary Depends on It

Ding! When the clock strikes the beginning of your business day, you should work as though your salary depends on it. After all, it does!

The difference between successful relationship-developers and those who "talk a good game" is that the first group is busy making rain while the other group is talking about doing it.

When I launched my business, I wasn't smart enough to be scared. I didn't realize the risks involved in running a firm. Luckily for me, I also had not read the statistics that a high percentage of start-up companies fail within the first few years. What I did know, however, was that success is a mind-set. I knew that it required putting your left foot in front of your right foot and making each minute in the business day count.

Making each minute count means dealing with personal errands during the workday only if the office or store you are calling is closed after your organization's business hours. It also means discouraging family members and friends from contacting you at work when they can just as easily leave a message for you on your residential telephone line or in your personal e-mail box.

Working as though your salary depends on it means having a plan for each and every workday. It means doing whatever it takes to accomplish your plan or move it forward. And it means holding yourself to a higher standard than any manager would ever hold you.

Here's why this is so important. When prospects and clients recognize your work ethic, they are more likely to respect you and want to work with you. After all, most clients see vendors as an outsourced part of their team. Who wouldn't want to give their business to someone who takes her career seriously enough to work as though her salary depended on it?

Courtship Tips

1. Work as though your salary depends on it.

2. Recognize that your strong work ethic will be appreciated by prospects.

What People Really Want Are the Basics

When my 28-year-old son took a job with an established company, he quickly noticed that most of his clients were at least 20 years older than he was.

When most of his clients met him, they appeared to be uneasy because of his age and lack of industry experience. Their skepticism was quickly dispelled, however, when they asked him point-blank how long he had been in the "field."

"I've been in this field a very short time," he said. "For that reason, I'm counting on you to ask the right questions. In fact, I want to know that I really only know three things."

"Really?" the client would ask. "And what are the three things you do know?"

Here's what he would say in response:

1. "I know how to be honest."
2. "I know how to give a fair price."
3. "I know how to be responsive, and that includes returning your telephone calls promptly."

More often than not, his new clients would say, "It sounds like you have what it takes to handle our business. Welcome aboard."

When you practice *and* preach the basics—honesty, fairness, and responsiveness—your prospects and existing clients will know that *their* priorities are *your* goals. Everything else is secondary.

Courtship Tips

1. Tell people what you do know rather than what you don't know.

2. Empower your prospects by letting them know you are counting on them to ask the right questions.

3. Be honest, give fair prices, and be responsive.

Communication Is Everything!

Some of the most brilliant people have failed miserably in business due to their lack of communication skills.

Here's a story that illustrates what I mean. A very smart man with a background in technology was in the process of being promoted to manager. The woman to whom he would be reporting, however, felt that he lacked the appropriate interpersonal relationship skills for managing a team. When she called my company to seek help for her new direct report, my first question was, "Is this person open to enhancing his interpersonal relationship skills?"

Her automatic response was, "If he isn't, he won't be promoted. It's as easy as that. This area of concern has been addressed with him, so I'm quite sure he will be open to it."

We discussed potential dates to meet. Once an appointment was set, an e-mail assessment was sent that both this technology professional and his manager were asked to complete. The goal of this assessment was for each of them to compare and contrast how they each rated this soon-to-be promoted person's interpersonal relationship skills.

Two weeks after the initial phone calls, the first consultation took place in our conference room. As I expected, the gentleman arrived a few minutes before our scheduled meeting and was a person of few words. When I asked him why he thought we were meeting, he responded, "My new boss. She's just like my wife. She talks, talks, talks, talks, talks. I'm a person who likes to make my point and move on. I'm just the opposite."

I put on my neurolinguistic cap. It was apparent that this technology person processed information in visual terms. His spouse and recently appointed manager related in a feeling, also called *kinesthetic* manner just as I had expected. I said to him, "I see what you mean about the communication barriers. If you saw there was a way to figure out how to talk so that they would listen to you, would you do it?"

"Yes," he said.

"Well, here goes. Whenever you talk with your manager or spouse, simply say three things more than what you would normally say. For instance, are you planning on calling your manager when you leave this coaching session?"

"How did you know that's what she asked me to do? She dropped me an e-mail that read: 'As soon as you've left the coaching session, leave me a voice mail to let me know how the consultation went.'"

"The question is," I pressed, "*What are you going to say when you phone her?*"

He replied, "I'm going to say that the coaching was fine and that I'll see her at our 3 p.m. meeting."

"Hmmm," I said. "Think about how she perceives your communication style as lacking people skills. She wants to hear much more than the facts from you. She wants emotion. She wants you to use superlatives like she does. This is quite typical of kinesthetic people. If you see that you'd like our consultation to be the one and only coaching session, try this. Say three more things than you would normally say to her and I promise she will perceive you as more outgoing and possessing the people skills she keeps talking about."

"If I do as you say, will you promise I won't have to return for another consultation?" he asked.

He was starting to like this game, I noticed.

"If you continue to implement what we are discussing, I promise," I said.

"All right," he said. "Let's see."

"So what are you going to say?" I asked.

He thought for a moment, took a deep breath, and said, "Good morning, Mary. I hope you're having a great day. The consultation went very well. I look forward to seeing you at the 3 p.m. meeting. Bye now."

Then he made an "I think I'm going to be sick" face. Yet that was just his sense of humor. I could tell that he got it.

As we parted ways, I congratulated this person for catching on to the power of neurolinguistics so quickly.

Apparently he saw the value of it. Two weeks following the consultation, his manager called me and said, "I don't know what you did to that man, however he's so much more outgoing. Thank you."

The moral: Identify the other person's communication style and try your best to match it, even if it feels odd at first to do so.

I promise, you'll be glad you did!

Courtship Tips

1. You're only as good as what the person observing you believes you are.

2. Put yourself on others' neurolinguistic wavelengths by speaking their lingo.

Keep Track of Your Communication With Prospects

If you want to grow prospect relationships, you have to monitor the courtship process. The simple tracking system that follows can be part of a contact management program, yet it can also be adapted with relative ease to any word processing or database program. This system allows you to track each and every prospect with whom you have had communication, when and how you connected the person, and the date of each communication.

This organizational tool can act as a road map for where you are in the relationship development process at any given time. It will also help you stay "in the loop" with those relationships that seem to take an eternity to develop.

3-9-04	**Insurance Company**	513-555-1212	Mark Noble

436 Gale, Cincinnati, OH 45236

Mark.Noble@insurancecompany.com

Mark contacted us after reading an article in the newspaper.

E-mailed information to Mark about our programs.

Sent the information packet to Mark along with a copy of the blue 101 ways.

Confirmed delivery.

Added Mark to the Tip of the Month log.

3-24-04 E-mailed Mark to let him know another client is interested in
August 4, 5, and 6.

3-25-04 Mark e-mailed requesting July 14, 15, 21, or 22.

E-mailed Mark to let him know I will keep July 14 and July 15 penciled in.

Scheduled time to visit with Mark over the phone. Friday, March 26 or
Wednesday, March 31.

3-31-04 Spoke with Mark and Anna about our programs

Penciled in July 14 and July 15 to work with their team.

Added Anna to the corporate excel list.

4-7-04 E-mailed Mark to learn if he would like to secure July 14 and 15 (another client
is interested in July 14).

Follow up with Mark on April 16 to learn of their decision (they should have
one by the middle of the week).

4-16-04 E-mailed Mark to learn if they would like to secure July 14.

5-18-04 Mark e-mailed to secure July 21, 2004.

Sent Mark the contract to secure July 21 from approximately 8:00 a.m. to
2:00 p.m.

Communication 1

3-9-04	**XYZ Bank**	239-555-1212	Terri Allen

624 Smith Rd., Naples, FL 33109

tallen@xyzbank.com

Terri contacted us about our on-site programs for her team.

E-mailed the most commonly requested program topics to Terri.

Followed up with Terri to make sure she received the info that we sent.

Mailed the originals to Terri along with a copy of the book.

5-25-04 Terri called to confirm receipt of the material.

Added Terri to the Tip of the Month log.

6-3-04 Spoke with Terri. She is interested in scheduling multiple programs for
various offices.

Sent a revised proposal to Terri for working together.

Marked the calendar to call Terri on June 15 to learn how they would like
to proceed.

6-16-04 E-mailed Terri to learn if they would like to reserve three programs for
their various offices.

Terri faxed back the signed agreement for securing three programs in 2004.

Communication 2

Leave a Good Paper Trail

Superior relationship-developers recognize the value of paying attention to detail. They know that dotting the i's and crossing the t's also means documenting each and every prospect and client communication.

They keep such a thorough paper trail that they can be away from their offices for an extended period of time without missing a prospect or client beat. Courtship-focused rainmakers who have a personal assistant treat this person as a partner by empowering him or her to make decisions based on past precedent.

Those who do not have a support person arrange to have their colleagues handle their prospect and client communication. In turn, they cover for that individual when they are on vacation or are elsewhere for an extended period of time.

Truly effective rainmakers know they are not indispensable. They keep such outstanding, well-organized prospect and client records that virtually anyone can retrieve information they need within minutes and be able to pick up prospect/client communication where it left off. These relationship-developers know that good organization is a great way to impress prospects and clients.

Courtship Tips

1. Make it easy to remember your last communication with prospects. Get organized by documenting each and every communication.

2. Recognize that prospects will be impressed when someone on your team can pick up the conversation where you left it, whether it be two days or two years after the fact.

3. Empower others to handle your communication when you are going to be out of reach for any length of time. Make the job easy for them by getting and staying organized.

Design a Business Courtship Plan That Will Work With Your Prospects

The best thing about a contact management system is that it allows you to pick up your next communication where you left off the last time you were in touch with that person. You also will be able to document the history of what it takes for this prospect to make decisions.

Start the list by documenting the date of the initial contact. Add the individual's name, address, phone number, and e-mail address.

Add notes about what you discussed, any deadlines that have to be met, or dates you may be meeting with them.

Our contact management system tracks the progress of our prospects based on their neurolinguistic communication patterns. Following, you will see three examples: one of the prospect who tends to make quick decisions (visual); one of the prospect who needs to analyze the information carefully and schedule several meetings to discuss its value (auditory); and one of the prospect who may take a year or two before making a decision (kinesthetic).

7-12-04	**Local Organization** 513-555-1212		Dan Bevins

68 Melvin Ave., Cincinnati, OH 45202

Dan.Bevins@local.com

Dan left a message on voice mail about on-site programs for his teams.

Spoke with Dan about the pricing for on-site sessions.

7-16-04 Followed up with Dan.

Sent a proposal for working together on September 16, 2004.

Offered to hold the date until July 29.

Marked the calendar to follow up on July 29, 2004, to learn how he would like to proceed.

The Visual Prospect

| 3-13-04 | **SSS Bank** | 415-555-1212 | Jamie Marks |

514 Main St., San Francisco, CA 90013

Jamie_S_Marks@sssamro.com

Jamie called our company after Ann Marie's name was brought up in a meeting.

The bank is looking at options for a program with a meal or without a meal for Banking Center Managers.

E-mailed Jamie the most commonly requested programs.

Scheduled to speak with Ann Marie on Friday, March 14.

3-14-04   Left a message for Jamie to schedule a date—possibly in June.

Offered June 4, 9, or 12.

Spoke with Jamie about the training. She will keep us posted.

Quoted a specific amount for training up to 30 individuals.

Added the bank president to the corporate excel list.

5-14-04   Jamie called our firm. She is interested in June 5 or 12, July 9 or 10, or August 5.

She's looking at a program from approximately 8:00 a.m. to noon.

5-21-04   Called Jamie to let her know that we still have June 12, July 10, or August 5 available for her.

Send the letter of engagement to Jamie to secure August 5, 2004.

The Auditory Prospect

| 1-9-04 | **Investment Firm** | 617-555-1212 | Angie Anis |

75 Middle St., Boston, MA 06713

AAins.1@investment.com

Angie contacted our firm after receiving the January Tip of the Month.

1-10-04   Spoke with Angie and sent the information packet, along with the 101 ways book.

1-15-04   Met with Angie at her office in Boston.

1-27-04   Left a voice mail for Angie to learn how we may work together.

2-7-04   Left a voice mail for Angie to learn where they are in their decision.

4-10-04   E-mailed Angie to see if she would like to meet for breakfast the week of April 14.

4-11-04   Angie e-mailed back. Marked the calendar to contact her the first week in September to learn how we may work together.

9-10-04   E-mailed Angie to learn how we may work together. Angie e-mailed back to let us know that they would like a pilot program. Possibly in November or December.

9-11-04   Left a message for Angie to let her know the pricing for a Lunch 'N Learn.

9-17-04   Left a message for Angie to let her know that we could present a pilot program for their group in mid-October, when I will be working with a university in the area.

9-23-04   Sent Angie a proposal for working together in March 2004.

The Kinesthetic Prospect

Exercise

Contact Management Pages

Directions: Make a list of your prospects to determine if they are visual, auditory, or kinesthetic.

My *VISUAL* prospects include:

1. _____
2. _____
3. _____
4. _____
5. _____
6. _____
7. _____
8. _____
9. _____
10._____

The last five times I heard from them, they communicated with me via:

1. _____
2. _____
3. _____
4. _____
5. _____

My *AUDITORY* prospects include:

1. _____
2. _____
3. _____
4. _____
5. _____
6. _____
7. _____
8. _____
9. _____
10. _____

The last five times I heard from them, they communicated with me via:

1. _____
2. _____
3. _____
4. _____
5. _____

My *KINESTHETIC* prospects include:

1. _____
2. _____
3. _____
4. _____
5. _____
6. _____
7. _____

8. _____

9. _____

10. _____

The last five times I heard from them, they communicated with me via:

1. _____

2. _____

3. _____

4. _____

5. _____

Remember:

Your *visual* prospects will communicate with you *in writing* on a normal basis.

Your *auditory* prospects will usually *call* you.

Your *kinesthetic* prospects will be people of *many words* and *spontaneous* individuals.

Courtship Tips

1. Create a contact management system that works for you.

2. Track your prospects' relationship development behaviors.

3. Compare and contrast what it takes for different prospects to sign on with you.

Always Ask Permission for Others' Time

Before I started to write books, I began writing weekly newspaper columns. In order to be asked to write, however, I had to pitch the columns...and they had to be accepted!

The way my business etiquette column was picked up by the *Life!* section of the *Washington Times* was a lesson in itself. I was in Washington having breakfast at the Mayflower Hotel. As I was waiting for my meal to arrive, I was reading the *Washington Times*. When I got to the *Life!* section, my sixth sense told me that my column belonged there. Immediately after breakfast, I called the *Washington Times* to learn the name of the *Life!* editor. The receptionist also mentioned that it was his first day in the position.

Most people would have left the poor guy alone for a week or two until he settled into his new job. For some reason, however, it seemed my knowing that this person had just assumed the role of editor was working in my favor. My premise was that new editors often like to introduce new topics to their readers.

The challenge was getting him to answer his line. Finally, at 6:30 p.m., John Podhoretz picked up his line. "John Podhoretz," he answered.

"Mr. Podhoretz, congratulations on your first day on the job. This is Ann Marie Sabath, a self-syndicated columnist," I said. Then I asked confidently, "Would you give me a minute?"

"You have one minute," he replied.

"Mr. Podhoretz, I was reading the *Life!* section today and see that my business etiquette column would be a perfect fit. I'd like to have three sample columns in your hands tomorrow morning. Would that be acceptable?"

Although his to-the-point reply was "yes," I wasn't sure if he was slightly interested or just wanted to end the call after a long first day.

By 10:30 a.m. the following morning, Mr. Podhoretz received a Federal Express package with a cover letter, three sample columns, and two letters from editors for other publications where my column appeared.

One week later I placed a follow-up call to him, and he expressed his interest in picking up the weekly column. I am convinced that this long-term business relationship was due to my respect for his time on the phone and to that special question I asked with confidence: *"Would you give me a minute?"*

And let's face it: seizing the moment played a big role, too.

Courtship Tips

1. Seize the moment. When it feels right—do it!

2. Always ask for permission to talk before jumping into a conversation with a new contact.

3. Ask new contacts confidently, "Would you give me a minute?"

The Early Bird Catches the Worm: Adapt Your Schedule to the Time Frame of Your Prospects and Clients

Be ready to get together with prospects on a moment's notice. In other words, if a prospect calls you at the last minute and your schedule permits you to meet, do so!

One of the founders of a 50-year-old law firm told his young lawyers about how he acquired a client company during the firm's first year in business:

The president of a small uniform company based in the suburbs contacted three law firms located in the heart of the city. He let them know that he was "shopping" for legal counsel.

The partners of the first two law firms asked this prospect to let them know when he would be downtown so they could meet him. The partner of the third firm, the man telling the story, responded in a different manner. He asked the president of this uniform company when he would like to meet. The president's response was, "What about now?" The partner said, "I'll be there in 45 minutes."

Guess who got the business?

The partner who was ready, willing, and able to be responsive to this prospect landed the account. This small uniform company grew into a multimillion-dollar business. If only the other two law firms had been responsive, they might have given the third law firm a run for its money. Instead, this attorney, who was savvy enough to adapt his schedule to the needs and wants of this prospect, won the business hands down. The great news is that this uniform company has remained its client for more than 44 years!

The next time a prospect appears interested in meeting, try asking, *"When would you like to meet?"* This question could open a door for you and the organization you represent that could lead to a long-term client.

Courtship Tips

1. Ask not when you may meet with prospects. Ask prospects when they would like to meet with you.

2. Recognize that the early bird really does catch the worm. Schedule meetings for sooner rather than later.

Educate and Inform...and Watch Business Come to You

When you create a strategy to educate and inform your prospects, they will eventually do business with you.

Many courtship-focused dealmakers create innovative courtship experiences in the form of lunch or dinner seminars. They select a location that is a "draw" for prospects and recognize that only a certain percentage of those invited prospects will attend. However, the best rainmakers also recognize that some of the individuals who attend are bound to become clients over time.

Let me give you a specific example of how this works. One year after opening our Manhattan office, I identified the target market of organizations that would most likely be attracted to our firm's client relationship programs. I drew this conclusion based on the one organization that our firm had attracted as a client. This firm was one of the top 25 firms we had been trying to acquire.

Since this client relationship had become a solid one, my goal was to develop similar relationships with several of the other target firms. My thought was to offer a "Put Your Best Fork Forward" Lunch 'N Learn Program for the recruiting directors of each of the prospect firms. I ran the idea by my first client to see if she thought this idea would be accepted by her counterparts in other firms. She thought it was a great idea, and she also mentioned that the W Hotel in Times Square had recently opened and might be a terrific draw for this Lunch 'N Learn Program.

I took her advice and met with the hotel. Four weeks prior to the scheduled Lunch 'N Learn date, we sent out invitations to each prospect, accompanied by a small gift box containing a sterling silver-plated fork wrapped in beautiful silver foil. The gift boxes containing the forks were sent with the invitations to differentiate this mailing campaign from other pieces of mail that these prospects would receive that day.

Sure enough, R.S.V.P.s started pouring in by fax and phone. We were pleasantly surprised to realize that what we viewed as a marketing strategy was seen by our clients as "an event"—which is, of course, as it should be! In fact, two firms that were not on our list contacted *us* and asked to be put on the invitation list! We were thrilled at this interest and welcomed them to the luncheon.

On the day of the R.S.V.P. deadline, we reviewed the list of individuals who were attending and those who had not yet responded. A personal telephone call was made to each person who had not yet responded. Although some event planners may have seen this follow-up as a waste of time, we found that one person had faxed her response, which had not been received; another had just returned from out of the country and had not opened her mail; and so forth. The bottom line was that by the time the follow-up calls were complete, we saw that each and every one of the top firms that received our "Put Your Best Fork Forward" Lunch 'N Learn invitation would be represented at our two-hour event.

Because we saw these invitees as hot prospects, we began courting them like no other. They were sent confirmations five days prior to the event as a gentle reminder to keep this date on their calendar. This follow-up also was part of the "prospects have to see things seven times to react" closing campaign.

The day of the event arrived. Every i was dotted and t was crossed. We planned to make the two hours both fun and informative. As individuals stepped off the elevator on this warm spring afternoon, they were greeted by one of the hotel personnel who directed them to the room. A server met them in front of the room with a glass of Perrier. Once they were in the room, I greeted them and thanked them for taking time from their busy schedules to join us. As the clock struck noon, each person was invited to be seated where the tent listing their name and organization was found. Our existing client was gracious enough to introduce us and share how her team had benefited from our client relationship training.

The two hours flew by. As individuals enjoyed the hotel's cuisine, they were taken through "The Art of Entertaining During Business Meals," followed by "Strategies for Making Your Net Work for You During Receptions and in Other Unstructured Settings." Each invitee was asked to share what she/he found to be of most interest from the program. Evaluations were distributed to everyone, along with little gifts from Tiffany, Godiva, and Takashimaya to those who returned the sterling silver forks. (Because the most challenging part of this campaign was securing these forks from antique stores, we wanted them back so we could reuse them for other "Put Your Best Fork Forward" Lunch 'N Learn Programs.)

As soon as the event was over and we bid each person adieu, the comments were reviewed and then compiled in an evaluation summary form. Each attendee was sent a letter of thanks, along with a summary of what participants said about the program.

Although each firm was represented, a few of the decision-makers had fill-ins from their team attend. Since we wanted to reinforce directly to them which organizations were represented and how their counterparts benefited from the program, we created a "We Missed You" letter. The evaluation summary was enclosed with this follow-up.

Yes, this marketing campaign was a lot of work, however it paid off. During the next six months, four of the firms represented became clients. One year later, two more of the firms we had invited hired us.

Educate and inform—and watch business come your way!

Courtship Tips

1. Keep your name in front of your target audience.

2. Once your targeted prospects have seen you seven to 10 times, schedule a special event for them.

3. Make it stand out! Make it an event!

4. Educate and inform.

5. Follow up and follow through.

Make Your Net Work for You

One secret to successful courtship lies in understanding that your existing clients must be so *wowed* by their interaction with you that they share your name with someone who could also benefit from your expertise. This is by far the highest compliment you will ever receive in the business world!

Whenever this happens, be sure to drop your raving fan a handwritten thank-you note. Besides displaying your attention to detail, this strategy will ensure that the person becomes your ambassador for life!

Courtship Tips

1. Please your existing clients and they will create business opportunities for you.

2. Send a handwritten thank-you to your raving fan. A written thank-you has much more impact than a verbal one.

Own Up!

When a prospect or client complains about something, what is your typical response?

Does what you say sound like this: "You're right. That *other* department is really screwed up"?

Or do you acknowledge what you heard with a "thank you" and then "own" the situation by telling the person what you *can* do about the situation?

Successful courtship-focused rainmakers go above and beyond by *owning* complaints rather than closing their eyes to them. They interpret constructive criticism as feedback for bettering themselves and their organizations.

Rainmakers know how to convert complaints into opportunities. They do so by either resolving the problem or creating a new system to prevent the situation that caused the client to complain from occurring again.

Successful rainmakers recognize that talk is cheap. They have learned from experience that *documentation encourages people to take action.*

Prospects and existing clients really do measure an organization's success on how a situation is handled rather than the situation that caused the complaint in the first place.

Courtship Tips

1. When prospects and existing clients voice complaints, take ownership of their concerns—no matter how busy you are.

2. Remember, the way a complaint is handled impacts prospects and clients more than whatever caused the person to complain in the first place.

The Art of Preplanning Meetings

What do you do to go above and beyond when preparing for prospect meetings?

While most dealmakers arrive early with presentation material in hand, here is what a few savvy rainmakers do for going above and beyond:

1. A confirmation is sent to prospects via e-mail or snail mail thanking the person for scheduling the upcoming meeting. This correspondence includes a summary of what the rainmaker would like to learn about each prospect's interests and needs during the meeting. Besides putting thoughts

on paper, they are giving their prospects time to prepare answers for what will be asked of them during the scheduled get-together.

2. When more than four people will be part of a scheduled meeting, savvy rainmakers prepare name tents (that is, place cards listing people's names and organizations). Besides being a way of remembering names, they know most people like seeing their name in print. Name tents subconsciously give people a sense of belonging.

3. A savvy rainmaker also takes the liberty of preparing an agenda. If this is a first or second informational meeting, there is a good chance the prospect has not had an agenda prepared. It goes without saying that an agenda is a great way of ensuring that priority areas are addressed during the scheduled time.

Courtship Tips

1. Send prospects a confirmation via e-mail or snail mail. Include the areas that you would like to learn about the prospect's specific interests and needs.

2. Prepare name tents when four or more individuals who you will be meeting for the first time will be part of the scheduled meeting.

3. Prepare a meeting agenda. Besides helping you to keep the meeting focused, prospects will see the effort you made for preplanning the meeting.

The Ask, Don't Tell Principle

Professionals who know the true sense of client relationship development have mastered the power of listening. They live by the "Ask, Don't Tell" principle.

Savvy rainmakers know that by following this principle, prospects are more likely to see them as *interesting*. Remember, you will be seen as more *interesting* when you are *interested* in others. These successful professionals also recognize the value of offering information about themselves when asked.

In addition, these rainmakers know how to position what they want to say with a question about the topic they would like to address.

Example: Joe is really looking forward to playing the course at Pinehurst. Rather than saying that, however, he asks one of his prospects, who is an avid golfer, "Have you played at Pinehurst?"

No matter what the person responds, Joe can build on the response by saying, "Our quarterly meeting is scheduled there. I'll let you know how our team enjoyed it.

Courtship Tips

1. Ask, don't tell.

2. You will be seen as more interesting when you are interested in others.

News Flash: You Act Like You Look, and You Get Results Based on How You Dress

The way you dress determines both how you act and how others perceive you.

Prospects interpret the quality of service you provide by how you package yourself. When wearing appropriate attire, they will see you as looking as though you mean business. And when you're dressed professionally, *you* see yourself as looking as if you mean business, too!

On a recent trip to Salt Lake City Airport, my driver and I struck up a conversation. When I asked him how long he had represented the car service, he said two years. He had been a high school principal and missed the people contact after retiring.

I asked this soft-spoken professional his opinion on student dress codes in the high school arena during the past several years. His comments were enlightening. He told me that students conformed to what was both expected of them and enforced. He reinforced his belief by sharing that each year his high school's graduating class went to Disneyland. They knew that in order to have fun with Mickey, they had to abide by the dress code expectations that Disneyland has. These seniors also knew better than to resist Disneyland's dress code, knowing they would not be admitted into the park if they didn't play by the rules!

Why does Disneyland instill dress restrictions? They realize that when high standards are enforced, they will be maintained. The individuals representing this world-renowned theme park also recognize that proven results demonstrated that their dress code resulted in better park behavior.

What lessons are there for us in the Disneyland example? How does what we wear affect the way others perceive us, the way we perceive ourselves, and the responses we receive in the business world?

Prospects will equate the attention you pay to your dress to the detail you pay in the service you would like to provide them. And *you* will act, think, and communicate differently when you are dressed for success than when you aren't!

When in doubt, dress a notch higher than you expect your prospects to dress.

People who look the part are more likely to accomplish their goals. When they choose not to look as though they mean business, their requests often are discounted.

One of my bank clients who was dressed in business casual had a client drop by his office. Because the bank had only recently instituted business casual attire, the client commented in surprise about the dress code change. He said, "Now that you'll be dressing casually, is that how you'll be treating my money?"

Good question!

Whether your prospects and clients express this concern aloud, you can be sure some of them are asking themselves this question.

Another program participant explained that he consistently is treated differently by store clerks when he's dressed in business attire vs. a jogging suit. He explained that a few holiday seasons ago, he went to a department store to exchange a few items. He was wearing a jogging suit and was scrutinized by the store clerk at his request to return the items he had received as gifts. This person mentioned that he also noticed that the man in front of him who was also exchanging holiday gifts was treated much better by the same store associate. The only difference was that the customer treated better was wearing a suit.

The following year when he went to the department store to once again exchange a few items, he intentionally wore a suit. It worked. He was treated with more respect than he had been treated the previous year.

Courtship Tips

1. The way you look determines how prospects perceive both you and the service you represent.

2. Your attire also affects the way you see yourself, and in some cases the way you perform on the job.

3. Set the tone by the dress expectations for yourself and those around you.

4. Dress one notch higher than you expect your budding rainmakers to do.

Court Prospects the Costco Way

If you have been to Costco, then you already know that shoppers who walk in with grocery lists more often than not leave the store with much more than they had intended to buy.

Why is that?

This warehouse-like store is known for its bulk packaging, yet the reason people buy the unexpected has to do with "the Costco experience."

During the peak hours, Costco has tasting tables in prominent places. The individuals at these tables are knowledgeable about the food or other item they represent. In turn, a food or product sample frequently prompts a sale of the last thing you planned to buy.

Whenever possible, take the lead from Costco by giving your prospects a "taste" of the service or product you represent. Prospects will appreciate the extra effort you are making by this experiential treatment of your services.

Courtship Tips

1. Create a chance for your prospects to experience firsthand the service or product you represent.

2. Give prospects a sample when possible.

3. Give prospects more than what they expect.

Keep Prospects Updated

Courtship-focused rainmakers let prospects and existing clients know exactly what they can count on in the immediate future. Specifically, they keep the lines of communication open by treating their voice-mail box as though it is a live personal assistant.

When was the last time you were prepared to leave someone a voice-mail message only to hear a message with an "I'm not available?" This type of message only keeps callers in the dark.

What about the time you called someone and got an update about when you could count on a return call? For instance: "This is George Smith. Please leave your name, number, and message. I will return your call this afternoon upon returning from Tuesday morning meetings." Talk about a better impression.

Courtship-focused rainmakers who know how to make their voice-mail boxes work for them update their messages regularly. They realize that this automated tool can be as effective as a live personal assistant when it is used properly.

If you have any say in how telephone calls are routed, I strongly suggest that you find a way to get a live human being to answer the line. This personal touch can be the difference between prospects doing business with you or your competition.

Be sure to update your voice-mail message. The best way to turn off a caller is for the person to hear your updated message from Monday on Tuesday. Many people avoid updating their message for fear of forgetting to change their message. My response to them is, "You remember the day you get paid. You certainly can remember to update your voice-mail message." The secret is to do it at a specific time as a matter of habit— either at the end of the day or first thing in the morning.

Courtship Tips

1. Update your voice-mail message regularly. State when you'll be able to return the message.

2. Whenever possible, give callers a chance to speak to a live human being before their call is routed to your voice-mail box.

Build a Brain Trust—and Play With Prospects a Little

Nine months after our corporation was founded and 60 telephone calls and follow-up letters later, the *Cincinnati Enquirer* picked up my column.

With a Gannett newspaper under my belt, I thought that convincing other papers would be a cinch! *Wrong!*

Alan Kelley was the man I began courting. He was the *Features* editor for the *Dayton Daily News*. Getting through to him was a challenge. Each time I placed a call to him, his very competent assistant would answer the line. She would explain that he was either in a meeting, ready to head out the door, or on a deadline. I finally asked if she would let him know that I would be sending a cover letter and sample columns for his *Features* section. She willingly agreed.

One week later, after sending background information to Alan Kelley, I placed a call to him once again. By this time, his assistant and I recognized each others' voices. Once again, I learned that Mr. Kelley was not available to take my call, so I asked Ms. Marsh, "What do you suggest I do to get through to him? I'll take any suggestion you have."

Her response was, "Well, he does get in at 7 a.m. on Tuesday mornings. Why don't you try him around 7:15 a.m.?"

At that moment, I realized that Ms. Marsh had become part of my "brain trust" group. She knew that I was sincere in trying to reach him. Her "off the record" recommendation was definitely worth a try!

The following Tuesday morning at 7:15 a.m., I did exactly what Ms. Marsh recommended. I placed a call to Alan Kelley. She was absolutely right. After one ring, I heard, "Alan Kelley."

I knew I had to make my point quickly, so I said, "Mr. Kelley, thank you for answering. This is Ann Marie Sabath, business manners columnist for the *Cincinnati Enquirer*, *Washington Times*, and the *Dallas Times Herald*. I'm calling to see what it is going to take to make my column available to your readers on a weekly basis."

His response was, "I received your samples. Why don't you stop in sometime when you're in Dayton so we can meet?"

We scheduled a time later that month. A confirmation letter went out thanking Mr. Kelley for his time. When our scheduled date arrived, I wasn't quite sure if I was looking forward more to meeting Mr. Kelley or to meeting Ms. Marsh, who was instrumental in putting the two of us together.

Mr. Kelley was complimentary about my columns and said that his readers might enjoy such a topic. He also told me he was looking at another person who also had expressed an interest in writing a similar column. As the meeting neared an end, I thanked Alan Kelley for his time and let him know that I would respect whatever decision he would soon be making.

As I left his office, I said to myself, *"Wonderful! Now what?"*

I had one last chance to leave a great impression, and that was in my follow-up thank-you letter. It was the second week of March, and St. Patrick's

Day was just around the corner. *"That's it!"* I thought. *"I'll play off St. Patty's Day. A person by the name of Kelley certainly might appreciate this gesture."*

Later that afternoon, I prepared a thank-you to Alan Kelley on bright green 8 1/2 × 11-inch quality paper with a matching envelope. It read:

Dear Mr. Kelley:

It was a pleasure meeting you today. Thank you again for taking time from your busy schedule to see me.

As you know, it takes more than the "luck of the Irish" to be successful in business today. I hope you will allow me to assist you in giving your readers that competitive edge through my business etiquette column.

Sincerely,

Ann Marie O'Sabath
Just For Today

I figured Mr. Kelley would either think I was clever—or conclude that I had gone off the deep end. Apparently it was the former, because soon after the letter was received, I heard from Ms. Marsh.

Mr. Kelley, she told me, wanted to welcome me aboard.

Courtship Tips

1. Talk is cheap. Send your prospects some thing they can read. Then follow up with them. They will take what you have to say much more seriously.

2. Build a brain trust. Get administrative as sistants on your team by asking them their recommendations.

3. Display good sportsmanship with your prospects by letting them know you'll re spect their decision to do business with you or your competition.

4. Play with your prospects by sending unique follow-up messages to them.

He Who Speaks First About Fees Loses

When courting business, remember this rule: *He who speaks first about fees loses.*

Especially if you are representing a high-end service, make a point of courting prospects by sharing the benefit of your service. Be responsive, follow through, and do whatever you can to help the person become a raving fan. Whatever you do, only bring up fees when you are asked to do so—and not before.

Today, prospects tend to look at three things, and they tend to look at them in this order:

1. *Responsiveness*: Do you do what you say you are going to do, even before you have promised?

2. *Quality*: If you are representing a much-needed service or product, you will have competition. *So how can you outclass them?* The answer is simple: consistently under-promise and over-deliver!

3. *Fees*: So there you go. Fees are the third thing prospects look for when deciding on a service provider. When a prospect starts negotiating, recognize that the person probably enjoys the bantering ritual. Also keep in mind that people who negotiate are usually

confident enough to do so because they have some leverage with this budget. Enjoy the bantering and allow the person to have the last word. (It's always better to add a service that you will provide than it is to discount your fees!)

Courtship Tip

1. Let your prospects bring up the topic of fees.

Always Confirm Receipt

It was 1992. I had been growing my company, At Ease Inc., for five years. Then things exploded: *USA Today* did a story featuring one of our clients putting their "Best Fork Forward." Because I was the presenter, our firm received the peripheral benefits of this great press.

The phone rang off the hook. If you can imagine, 80 prospects contacted our firm. Several of these prospects are still our clients today.

One of the telephone calls that came in as a result of this coverage was from the head of a major publishing operation. After he acknowledged reading about our firm in *USA Today*, he asked if I would like to write a book. I thought I was dreaming. "Well, of course," I said. "However, who are you?" He told me.

I asked if he could send me the list of books his company had published, and in turn I offered to send him a business etiquette book proposal by Thursday of the following week. Was I ever excited! I worked like a mad woman until the 10-page proposal was finished, and off it went via UPS Ground.

One week after the proposal was scheduled to be delivered, I placed a follow-up call to my new ally, the publisher. Because he allowed himself to be accessible to others, I reached him on the first try. I said, "Good morning, this is Ann Marie Sabath. If you have a few minutes, I wanted to see what you thought of the business etiquette book proposal I sent you."

He said, "What proposal?"

With a lump in my throat, I thought I was hallucinating. I continued, "Well, if you remember, you phoned me two weeks ago and asked if I would be interested in writing a book on business etiquette. I promised to send you a proposal by the following Thursday. I worked hard to prepare the proposal and sent it to you via UPS for delivery last Tuesday—two days earlier than promised."

He said, "I have not received a proposal from you."

I realized that I needed to remain focused about the reason for my call—for him to approve the proposal, so I said, "May I fax the 10-page proposal to you within the next 10 minutes?"

I was never in my life so pleased to hear the word "yes."

I faxed the proposal and made a follow-up call to confirm that the fax had gone through. Then I placed a call to UPS. Where in the world was the proposal I had so carefully sent? I soon learned that UPS had indeed done what they were supposed to do: they delivered the package by the scheduled time. It was still sitting in the warehouse, however, and had simply not made its way to the head of the company. (This is, I soon learned, an extremely common problem with companies that have mailrooms and warehouses.)

Did I fault the person in the warehouse for that mistake? Not in the least. I blamed myself for the lack of follow-through. I should have confirmed with the publisher's assistant that the UPS package had in fact been received and placed in his office.

Many pleasant royalty checks later, I continue to remember the lesson from this experience. You're not finished until you are certain that what you have promised is in the hands of the receiver. Always follow up and follow through.

Courtship Tips

1. Under-promise and over-deliver. If you promise information by Thursday, have it to the person earlier.

2. The only thing you have is your word. Always, always, always confirm the delivery of time-sensitive material with the person waiting to receive it!

3. Always keep a hard copy of what you sent within reach so that you can refer to it or resend it within minutes.

Become a Contributing Editor

Courting business means creating opportunities for your prospects to learn about your expertise. One of the most nonthreatening and credible ways to do this is by looking for opportunities to share your expertise in the form of an article, column, or quick tip. Oftentimes, trade publications will see your expertise as an added benefit for their readership. This is a win–win way for you to make your services known to prospects.

Most professionals shortchange themselves by believing their expertise may not be of interest to the publication they would like to pitch. Too many professionals, in my opinion, discount what they have to offer and don't even bother to submit sample articles or columns to their favorite publications.

Once you have identified the trade publication with which you would like to be affiliated, follow these guidelines:

1. Format your writing piece based on the articles or columns that appear in the publication. This will assist the person to whom your piece is submitted in recognizing that you are familiar with the layout of the publication.

2. Read the masthead of a recent issue of the publication to identify the managing editor. If a receptionist or assistant is available when placing your call, try to learn the best time to speak with the person you are trying to reach. Administrative personnel are valuable sources of knowledge and can assist you with timing your call.

3. Place your telephone call first thing in the morning or during the lunch hour. You just may catch the person you are trying to reach at his/her desk.

4. Have a few copies of the publication at your fingertips. This will allow you to refer to an article of interest and/or

how your proposed column/article will fit into a particular section.

5. E-mail or snail mail a copy of writing pieces you are submitting the same day your call is placed to the person. This will allow the managing editor to have a visual point of reference when returning your call.

If you are fortunate enough to get your writing piece accepted, be sure to over-deliver on deadlines. It is one of the best ways to build trust with an editorial staff.

I can assure you that your article or column will be a terrific indirect marketing opportunity with prospects. You will be surprised of the shelf life of anything in print. You also will be pleasantly surprised by the credibility you will gain by being affiliated with a professional publication.

Courtship Tips

1. Recognize the power of the pen or keyboard. Take advantage of opportunities to be a columnist in your trade publication of choice.

2. Create opportunities by sending the managing editors of professional journals your writing samples. Offer to be a fill-in guest columnist.

Find the Rhythm

There's a rhythm to courting prospects and clients. The challenge is in defining your tempo.

How do you do that, you ask?

Figure out the last time you successfully developed a working relationship with a prospect. What makes clients want to continue to work with you when they could easily go to a competitor?

Rather than attempting to hurry a relationship, recognize that courtship is an ongoing journey. Let your prospects operate in their modus operandi: their own preferred time frame. The best thing you can do to make sure you become their vendor of choice is simply to keep your name in front of them.

Remember: The average business relationship typically takes a minimum of seven contacts to initiate! And relationships that are "born" in a more accelerated time frame have a way of "dying" just as fast.

Courtship Tips

1. Recognize each prospect's decision-making patterns. This will help you project their future decisions.

2. Relationships that begin fast typically end quickly.

Interruption or Opportunity?

Do you interpret prospects' telephone calls as opportunities or interruptions? Whether you are speaking to one person or to a group of 100, you must learn to welcome questions—at least if you want to master the art of courting new business. When you involve prospects in your interactions, they are more likely to enjoy doing business with you—if their experience is pleasant.

Prospects are likely to contact you according to the manner in which they best process information. Use the way they "contact" you as an opportunity to identify their neurolinguistic communication wavelengths. This will reinforce the most effective way for communication with them in return.

For example, recognize that your *visual* prospects are likely to present what they have to say by summarizing their comments to you in writing.

Prepare to interact more spontaneously with your *kinesthetic* prospects than you would with visual prospects.

Finally, expect to hear from your *auditory* prospects by phone because they tend to be more open when they hear from you.

When you are initiating contact with prospects and existing clients, do so according to their neurolinguistic wavelengths. In other words:

- E-mail, fax, or send a formal letter to your visual prospects to get meetings scheduled.

- Arrange an activity with your kinesthetic prospects so you will be involved in something together.

- Lastly, call your auditory prospects to ask the person to give thought to a date that will work best with the person's schedule.

By tuning in to your prospects' listening wavelengths, they will see you as a good listener. They also will see that you are the provider of choice with whom they will want to do business.

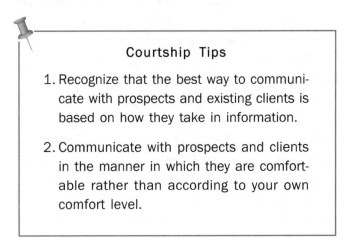

Courtship Tips

1. Recognize that the best way to communicate with prospects and existing clients is based on how they take in information.

2. Communicate with prospects and clients in the manner in which they are comfortable rather than according to your own comfort level.

You Are Only as Good as Your Own Team's Perception of You

When presenting business development programs, I frequently ask managers how their telephone lines are answered when they are out of the office. While many have their calls routed directly to voice mail, others have them answered by administrative staff.

During one training session, I asked participants whose line we could call to see how a team member handled a prospect's call. An individual by the name of Stephanie volunteered her office number because she had confidence that one of her competent team members would handle the call in a professional manner.

Stephanie was right. Within the second ring, a smiling voice was heard saying, "Good morning, XYZ Bank. This is Jennifer."

Without identifying myself, I asked if Stephanie was available.

Jennifer immediately explained that Stephanie was at an off-site meeting and would return to the office by 1:30 p.m. She maintained control of the call by asking if she could take a message or perhaps be of assistance to me.

I explained that it might be best if I left the message in Stephanie's voice-mail box, and then asked, "Is Stephanie good about returning calls?"

Jennifer said, "Sometimes."

I told her that rather than playing telephone tag, I'd call back later that afternoon.

Because we had arranged for the conversation to be put on speakerphone, when Jennifer spoke, everyone was mortified at her response. They too wondered how their teams would have responded to the last question I posed to Jennifer.

Stephanie handled Jennifer's comment in a most professional way. She said, "Even though I take pride in being responsive with clients, I must have done something to give Jennifer the impression that I do not always return calls promptly. You can be sure that I'm going to find out what it was so that my team feels confident telling callers that they can count on a call back from me by the end of each workday."

What impression do prospects and clients have regarding the way your line is answered?

Courtship Tips

1. Give individuals who answer your line both the responsibility and the authority to handle your calls.

2. Communicate your schedule to your team so they will be able to let callers know when to expect a returned call.

3. Recognize that your team is a reflection of you. Be sure to call your office to catch your team doing it right!

4. Make certain your department's line is answered promptly and properly by arranging "mystery calls."

Once You Earn the Business—Keep It!

One of the most common reasons that clients take their business elsewhere is the lack of service when service providers and vendors get lax or take their business for granted. Most organizations are set up so rainmakers have a support team to maintain the business once it is acquired. This in itself is dangerous.

Clients typically sign on with an organization because of the rapport established between the individual and the rainmaker. If your organization is set up to delegate business to an in-house team member shortly after it is acquired, you still have one major responsibility. You must contact clients a few times a month to confirm that they are in fact pleased with the level of service extended to them. By demonstrating your interest, you may save a client or two from slipping away. Your personal touch will remind the client why he/she choose your organization as the service provider or vendor of choice.

Finally, remember that the average piece of business takes a minimum of *six months* to acquire. It can be lost, however, in just a few seconds—the length of time it takes for a message to be mislaid, a call to be mishandled, or a mistake to be left unaddressed.

To err is human. To err in the same way repeatedly is professional malpractice.

Courtship Tips

1. Once you've converted a prospect into a client, remember that you are only as good as the individuals who are maintaining the business.

2. Check in with newly acquired clients at regular intervals to confirm they are receiving the "wow" service they deserve from your organization.

Ready, Set, Court!

Courting prospects is a three-step process:

1. Identify your target prospects.
2. Raise your prospects' level of awareness regarding the service you can provide to them.
3. Convert your prospects into clients by getting them to become clients.

Take a few minutes right now to identify all your new target prospects and then list how, specifically, you plan to expose them to the service you represent. Finally, list your strategies for converting them to clients.

	Target Prospect	Best Way to Introduce Your Service	Strategies for Converting Prospects to Clients
1.			
2.			
3.			
4.			
5.			
6.			
7.			
8.			
9.			
10.			

Courtship Tips

1. Remember: Courtship is a three-step process.

2. Strategize each step.

◆ Eight Courtship Pitfalls ◆

Following are eight common mistakes people make when trying to court new business. Avoid them!

1. Getting a prospect's voice mail and not leaving a message. (Most professionals now have phones displaying caller ID and know when you call.)

2. Believing a "no" means "no" when it really means "not now."

3. Believing that a verbal thank-you has the same impact as one that is written.

4. Using a sticky note for prospect communication rather than a note card or stationery with your organization's logo.

5. Communicating with prospects on your own neurolinguistic wavelength rather than in the manner in which they take in information.

6. Sending correspondence later than promised after learning that the prospect will

be out of the office on the day you said it
would arrive.

7. Not having an action plan regarding future
    contact as the last part of each communi-
    cation.

8. Not recognizing that prospects must see
    things seven times in order to react.

◆◆◆

Cutting In: Winning Prospects From Competitors

In business, it ain't over till it's over. You don't
have a client until the contract is signed.

Many times over the years, I have courted prospects for an extended period of time only to hear
them say, "We've been pleased with your responsiveness and see that you have a quality program,
however, we have selected another vendor."

While most people would feel rejected hearing those words, my staff and I have learned to
respond by saying, "Thank you for letting me know
that you've made the decision. I do have one question. Have you signed the contract with the other
vendor?"

Because I make a habit of remaining in close
contact with my prospects, the answer usually is
"not yet."

So I'm still in the game.

Consider the case of the pharmaceutical firm prospect that had contacted us for a proposal to train 1,200 of their reps during a national sales meeting. Laura was my contact—and also the bearer of the news that our firm had not been selected as the vendor of choice. (Cue violins.)

Laura and I had developed rapport through the business courtship process, so I asked her, "Laura, may I ask you what our firm could have done differently to be awarded this contract?"

Laura responded with, "When it was all said and done, the other organization was selected because our national sales manager has worked with them in the past."

I found that to be the most ridiculous reason in the world, so I said, "Laura, with all due respect to your national sales manager, that was a comfort decision, not an educated decision. Has the contract been signed?"

I could tell that Laura was beginning to squirm. She said, "I don't know."

I said, "Laura, is it possible for you to find out? I want to have a talk with your national sales manager before that contract is signed. In fact, I want to meet with him before he signs that contract. I'll be happy to hold if you could please let me know."

Although Laura was not the decision-maker, she definitely was my ticket in the door. We had established a strong level of rapport through our many telephone conversations and e-mail communications. That may be why she said, "If you don't mind holding a minute, let me check with Mr. Canning's assistant to see if the contract has been signed."

With bated breath I waited for Laura to return to the line, and then I heard her say, "The contract will be signed on Friday when our national sales manager returns from Anaheim."

"Laura," I said, "What's it going to take to meet with Joe Canning on Friday morning when he returns to the office before he signs that contract?"

At this point, Laura was very uncomfortable and said, "Ann Marie, the decision is in place and Mr. Canning is not one to change his mind."

"Laura," I pleaded, "please leave that up to me. If you could tell me the hotel where he is staying in Anaheim, I have an idea that will get him to see me on Friday morning."

At that point, Laura must have thought I was crazy. Yet we got along well, so instead of hanging up on me, she said, "Well, I do have a good relationship with his assistant. Let me find out. One moment, please." And she put me on hold once again.

Before long, Laura returned to the line and shared the Anaheim hotel where Mr. Canning was staying. Luckily for me, his meeting also was being held there the entire day.

"Laura, give me four hours and I will call you back. I have a feeling that what I'm going to do will encourage Mr. Canning to see me on Friday morning."

Three-and-a-half hours later, I called Laura once again. I asked her if she had word from Mr. Canning about what I sent him.

She said, "Apparently the stars are in your favor. He said he would see you at 8 a.m. on Friday— for one hour. What in the world did you send him to get him to agree to see you?"

After sighing a huge breath of relief, I explained to Laura that we had sent him flowers with the following poem:

Roses are red,
Violets are blue,
I hope you will let me
Do a pilot for you.

The following Thursday evening, I found myself sitting in the hotel room trying to figure out how I was going to convince Joe Canning that our firm should be the vendor of choice for their upcoming national sales meeting. If only I knew whether he was visual, kinesthetic, or auditory, then I could tailor my presentation to his learning style.

I then realized that the best thing to do would be to integrate all three styles into my 55-minute pilot program the following morning.

Here's how my thinking went.

If he is a "feeling" (kinesthetic) person, I must meet his sense of taste. Bagels and cream cheese it is. And yes, if he is a kinesthetic person, I just may have a decision at the end of the meeting.

If he is an auditory person, I must ask him how his return flight was so as not to push, knowing that auditory people give thought to what they hear before coming to a decision.

Finally, if Mr. Canning is visual, I must stay on track—so I'd better set up an airtight agenda.

The following morning, with bagels and an agenda in hand, I arrived at the pharmaceutical firm. After meeting Laura (a little gift for her in hand as a thanks for getting me in the door), I was escorted to the conference room. By 7:45 a.m., I was ready to meet with the man who I had to convince we were the training firm of choice.

The moment arrived. Mr. Canning entered the room. After greeting and thanking him for seeing me for an hour, I asked him about his return flight from Anaheim. As he was getting a bagel and cream cheese, he shared his feeling of jet lag.

I realized that the meeting was about to begin when Mr. Canning glanced at the agenda and then the box made of inlaid wood that I had placed in the middle of the conference-room table.

"What is this box doing in the middle of the table?" asked Mr. Canning. He fell for it—hook, line, and sinker.

"Mr. Canning," I said, "thank you for asking. I'd like to answer your question by sharing the 'Ode to Joe Canning' that I wrote for you last evening as I was gathering my thoughts for this morning's meeting."

An Ode to Joe Canning

Thank you for meeting with me today;
I know you are busy and have been away.
Laura, Betsy, and Connie certainly represent you well,
And by the end of this hour, I hope you can tell
That a relationship with our firm is the best decision
     you'll make.
Now let's begin talking to see what it will take.

You'll see I do what I love, and love what I do,
And my enthusiasm will soon rub off on you, too.
I guarantee that your reps and managers alike,
Will find our 10 sessions to be quite a delight.

They will learn, laugh, and role-play.
They'll e-mail me, too,
To say they've applied what they've learned
As soon as they are through.

Now what more do you want, accept perhaps a
     guarantee?
That's easy, just look on the agenda at item number three.

Now, Mr. Canning, would you want a rep to accept a
  "no" well,
Or turn it into a "yes" and continue to sell
Your products as I am pitching our training to you.
Please give me a chance, we'll do a superb job for you.

You may think that I'm nutty,
And that may well be;
However, I'm a terrific presenter,
Just wait and you will see.

When I finished, I saw the smile on Mr.
Canning's face so I continued. "Mr. Canning, to
answer your question about the box placed on the
table, this meeting is meant to represent an 'out
of the box' meeting. Here you are ready to hire a
training provider with whom you've worked.
That's an 'in the box' decision. My goal is for you
to make an 'out of the box' decision by hiring our
firm to assist you in making your national sales
meeting a success."

Mr. Canning said, "That's all fine and good;
however, we have made our decision."

"Mr. Canning," I continued, "may I ask you one
last question?"

He nodded, and I said, "Do your 1,200 reps
ever hear a 'no' from the physicians they are visiting?"

"Why of course," he said.

"Mr. Canning," I continued, "if you would like
them to continue to accept that 'no,' then you

should contract with the person with whom you are comfortable. If you would like your reps to learn, however, to turn a 'no' today into a 'yes' tomorrow, I recommend that you hire our firm. And here is a copy of the proposal for you to consider. Now Mr. Canning, what is it going to take to earn your business?"

Mr. Canning put down his coffee cup and stared at me. He finally said, "Ann Marie, do you really want our business that badly?"

"That's why I'm here, Mr. Canning. I want to know what it's going to take to earn your business."

Finally, Mr. Canning stood up and said to me, "You've earned our business, Ann Marie. As for this proposal, please revise it to include 1,200 of your books."

Courtship Tips

1. Recognize that it's not over until it's over.

2. Plan your meeting strategy according to the individual(s) with whom you will be interacting.

3. Build drama into your presentation.

4. Build your presentation around all three common communication styles.

Accommodate Prospects' Requests—Quick!

Many self-proclaimed rainmakers are slow to respond to their prospects. Either they are too busy or they wait to get back to prospects and clients until they have the complete answer.

Savvy, courtship-focused rainmakers, however, know that the accelerated time frame in which they respond to prospects is instrumental to clients selecting to do business with them. Successful rainmakers also know that every prospect must be treated as the most important one. They know that promptly acknowledging voice-mail or e-mail messages can be as important to prospects as the answer itself.

Unfortunately, some folks never learn the importance of quick response to the courtship process.

Courtship Tips

1. Responding promptly to prospects is sometimes more important than the answer itself.

2. Every prospect and client should feel as though they are the most important person in your world.

What Do Your Eyes Say?

Successful courtship-focused rainmakers project an air of confidence by the way they look when describing the service or product they represent. They speak with enthusiasm and maintain eye contact with prospects. They speak from their heart rather than from their head.

Look in the mirror as you are getting ready for work one morning. Do your eyes project the confidence to convince a prospect that he should invest in the service you represent?

If your eyes sparkle when you talk about the service or product you represent, you are probably seen as a person with passion for what you do. If prospects have a short attention span when talking with you, you may be speaking from merely your head rather than with your heart.

Courtship Tip

1. Be passionate about what you do. It shows, especially in the eyes.

Empower the Person Who
Answers Your Line

A business relationship is similar to a love relationship. You wouldn't want to marry someone you can't trust. Similarly, prospects want to do business with people who are accountable. They want to know when their calls are going to be returned.

If you have an administrative assistant, give the person both the responsibility to answer your line *and* the authority to either help callers or to schedule a specific time when you can return their calls. Administrative assistants should know your schedule *and* be empowered to schedule a specific time convenient for both you and your caller. Callers will appreciate knowing the specific time when they can expect a call back from you. And they'll also appreciate the reduced phone tag.

Courtship Tip

1. Empower your assistant by allowing the person to schedule specific times for you to return calls.

If You Cannot Return a Call by the End of the Day...

I was presenting a workshop for one of my law firm clients. Two of the three founding partners set the tone of the program with opening remarks to the young lawyers in this 50-year-old firm. One of the partners validated that it has always been and will always be the little things that continue to make a big difference in business. He explained that practicing law is secondary to how receptionists and partners alike treat clients. "If clients are not given outrageous service," he said, "what makes us believe we deserve their business?"

This partner explained to his young lawyers that the firm was founded on taking care of clients and that this premise was key for the firm to continue exceeding client expectations. His business development stories reinforced how critical it was to under-promise and over-deliver projects to clients and also what it takes for staying a notch above the competition.

By the time this savvy rainmaker finished his opening remarks, I felt like I had completed an accelerated workshop about what it takes to be successful in business. My favorite comment from this law firm partner, however, was when he talked about the importance of returning telephone calls.

As he stared pointedly at the future partners of his firm, he said, "If you can't return a telephone call by the end of the day, give it to me!"

Courtship Tips

1. It's the little things that continue to make the biggest difference in business.

2. Once you get the business, be ready to provide outrageously high levels of service to hold onto the business.

3. Return all calls by the end of the workday, even if that means simply acknowledging that the call has been received.

Woo Your Prospects With Notes

So often, people assume that a piece of business is secure once the ink is dry on a contract. What they forget is that the wooing and cooing must continue from this point forward. If the business is taken for granted, it's very possible for competitors to acquire the business.

One way to keep the courtship alive is by including a cover letter with documents that need to be signed. (I know many executives who give prepared documents to their assistants without requesting a short cover letter be attached explaining what is enclosed and welcoming the client to contact the person with any questions after reviewing the information.)

Courtship Tips

1. Remember: The wooing and cooing phase is still in place when the prospect turns into a client! It will continue for the life of the account.

2. Be sure your cover letter explains what the prospect is receiving.

Who Should Send the Thank-You When You Spring for Lunch?

Whoever initiates a business invitation picks up the bill, of course—that is, unless prospects or existing clients request a meeting over breakfast or lunch due to time constraints. In this particular case, a savvy rainmaker automatically picks up the bill.

Most professionals believe that the person paying the bill would have no need to send a thank-you note to guests later that day. A rain-maker who knows the real definition of courtship, however, knows that part of his relationship development strategy of keeping his name in front of prospects/clients means taking advantage of the opportunity to thank his guests for lunch.

People ask me, "Wouldn't a verbal or e-mail expression of thanks suffice?"

Perhaps for your competitors. A savvy rain-maker remembers that in order to accelerate business relationships as well as outclass your competition, it is essential to go above and beyond. The note should be sent via snail mail that day.

If e-mail communication is sent to the individual(s) who broke bread with you, so be it. While you might acknowledge how much you enjoyed visiting with the person(s) over the meal, let the thank-you note that has been mailed stand by itself. It's such an easy and effective way to keep your name in front of prospects and accelerate hearing those special words, *"We would like to do business with you."*

Courtship Tip

1. Whenever it takes a prospect or client more than 15 minutes to do something for you, a thank-you note is in order!

Cream Rises

Did you ever start to wonder if clients really notice who does what?

Say you're on a consulting project and you're working long hours on a tough problem. Your colleague, who also is on this project, schmoozes with your client like no other. This person, however, is not pulling her weight, which is making your part of the project more difficult.

There's something wrong with this picture. You are beginning to feel exploited.

If you have been in this situation, then you should know that everything—good or bad— eventually catches up with you. Just as cream rises, your work ethic and thoroughness will pay off in the long run.

Similarly, while clients and even managers may not say anything about your colleague's lackadaisical work behavior, it will eventually catch up with the person.

Avoid sabotaging your coworkers. This always backfires.

Whenever you find yourself in this type of situation, simply keep your nose to the grindstone. Pay attention to the details and show a little schmooze-ability yourself when the occasion arises!

Courtship Tips

1. Avoid sabotaging your coworkers. It always backfires.

2. Stick to your knitting. It will be noticed!

Tuck Them In

The written word is an important part of business courtship. Be sure all of your written communications conform to accepted grammar, spelling, and style standards.

When in doubt, ask someone you trust to proof your documents.

Tuck in those prepositions! While it may be considered acceptable for a preposition to be used at the end of a sentence when speaking (for example, "Who are you going with?"), this practice is frowned upon in formal documents. When asking the same question in written form, the question should be rewritten as: "Who will be joining you?"

Courtship Tips

1. The way you convey what you have to say is as important as the message itself.

2. Avoid using casual speech in your formal correspondence.

3. When in doubt, ask someone you trust to proof your documents.

Stop at the But! (And Other Lessons)

Winners find solutions. Losers make excuses.

When presenting business development programs, I ask people to identify words they should permanently delete from their vocabulary. One day when doing a training session, I asked the group why the word "but" should be removed from their word repertoire.

A young man quickly raised his hand and said, "People who use the word 'but' usually have an excuse following it."

Was he ever right!

"But" can act as a sound barrier for many people. When used, it can give the impression that whatever was said before it is being negated.

Another word to avoid using with prospects, clients, and anyone for that matter is "yeah." "Yeah" is perceived as a sloppy word and should be replaced with "yes." In order to get out of the habit of saying "yeah," simply repeat what you have said using "yes" as though you are reinforcing what you said.

Finally, the last word that should be deleted from your vocabulary is the word "think." I learned the value of deleting this word from the vocabulary of a client who had hired me to be part of his regional meeting. Following the program we were walking to the parking lot, and I said to my client, "So, Mr. DiAngelo, how do you think the program went today?"

Although I was expecting a compliment, I heard, "Ann Marie, do you really want to know?"

Surprised by his response, I said, "Yes."

"Ann Marie," began Mr. DiAngelo, "we did not hire you for you to tell us what you *think*. We hired you to tell us what you *recommend*, what you *suggest*, what you *believe*. Get the word 'think' out of your vocabulary. It's a weak word."

Surprised and humbled by his comment, I said, "Mr. DiAngelo, thank you for your candidness. I appreciate your perspective."

I hope you, too, will learn from Mr. DiAngelo's recommendation by using words of confidence— words with a backbone. Let your prospects and clients know you are a person of conviction by using strong words.

Courtship Tips

1. Replace "but" with "however."

2. Use "yes" rather than "yeah."

3. Use words of conviction, such as "recommend," rather than weak words such as "think."

Keep Your Eyes on the Target

Some people are naturals when it comes to accelerating business relationships. Here's my favorite example of this. It's a true story.

A woman wanted to work at a particular company located an hour away from where she lived. One day, she decided to drive to the firm to drop off her resume and perhaps complete an application.

She waited until the receptionist acknowledged her and then asked if she could leave her resume and perhaps complete an application for XYZ position. The receptionist informed her that the position in which she was interested was filled. She explained to this receptionist that she had traveled an hour and asked if she could please complete an application even though she understood that there were no available openings.

The receptionist seemed to find it easy to say "yes" to this person, perhaps because of her sincerity. Fifteen minutes later, with completed application in hand, the woman approached the receptionist and said, "When you have a few minutes, may I ask you one more question?"

"What is that?" replied the receptionist.

"I realize that the position for which I am qualified is not available, however, if it were open, what would be the next step?" asked the applicant.

"*If* the position were open, I would arrange for you to take a keyboarding test to check your speed and accuracy," said the receptionist.

The woman said, "Because I have traveled an hour, I would be most appreciative if you would allow me to take the keyboarding test. If the room where they test is occupied, I'd be happy to wait until it is available."

The receptionist said, "Well, I suppose it wouldn't hurt if you took the test. Let me call to see if the room is available."

Twenty minutes later, the woman found herself taking the keyboarding test. When she finished, she thanked the person who had administered it. She also thanked the receptionist who had been so cooperative by allowing her to complete the application and take the test.

The following morning, the woman, who had displayed more *chutzpah* that previous day than even she could ever imagine, received a telephone call. An employee resigned who held a position requiring similar skill that the applicant possessed. Because her application was on file, the personnel manager asked if she could come in for an interview.

When the woman told the story during one of my workshops, she also shared that she was offered the position and has been with the company for two years. After she started, she soon learned that the receptionist was the sister of the company owner, which gave her the clout to do the favors that had assisted this woman in landing the position.

When you want something, keep your eye on the target. Your goal can be accomplished with focus and gentle persistence.

Courtship Tips

1. Know what you want and go after it.

2. The *way* you ask for something is as important as what you ask.

3. What your mind conceives and you believe, you will achieve.

Does Failing Make You Bitter or Better?

Following one of my workshops, each person in the group was asked to complete an evaluation. Some participants said the program reinforced that courting business was a process. Others stated that they were reminded about the importance for prospects to encounter their service a minimum of seven times before expecting them to react. I was encouraged by this feedback and saw that each person had found the program to be time well spent.

Just as communication is a two-way street, so is training. In other words, I also learn from each program. In this session, my level of awareness was raised from a question asked by a participant on his evaluation. It read, "You shared your successes, and what about your failures?"

His question was a great one. In fact, it echoed in my ears for a few days. I kept asking myself, *"What, if anything, had I considered to be a failing situation? When had I felt as though I had fallen and could not get up?"*

How would you have answered that question?

I finally came to the conclusion that I have never thought of myself as failing. And I'm proud of that!

While many situations in my personal and professional life ended up differently than I expected, rather than perceiving them as "failures," I have considered them to be learning opportunities. I have found if you learn from a situation that has turned out differently than expected, there is no such thing as failure.

Courtship Tips

1. Recognize that all situations can be learning opportunities.

2. When you see yourself as having failed, get an AA (attitude adjustment).

Sink or Swim

It's when it looks like everything is falling apart that you have to be strongest.

I was staying in a historic hotel in a city where I had a program later that evening. Unfortunately, the term "historic" meant that it was old and shopworn and about half a century out of date. That evening it not only rained—it poured. I learned that this hotel was not only dated; it also leaked!

The following morning, I awoke to find two inches of water on the bathroom floor!

The water was steadily making its way to the bedroom. Because the hotel was sold out, my request to be moved to another room could not be met. I was quite upset...yet I tried to be positive.

I knew that business must go on. The workday started and my assistant transferred calls to me as I sat at the desk in my hotel room, watching the water seep closer.

"Something good has to happen," I thought.

I decided to place a call to the director of recruiting at the New York law firm that had requested a proposal for a Summer Associate Program. Their planning meeting had taken place the day before and I was optimistic that our firm had been selected as the training resource of their choice.

I was thrilled to hear the person pick up her line, and soon learned that their committee was in fact very impressed with our training programs. Unfortunately, that was the only good news. Another provider had been selected. I was quite disappointed and knew it was time to sink or swim. Because I felt that I had nothing to lose, I asked, "I really want your business. What will it take to earn it?"

My contact paused and then explained that our fees were slightly higher than the other organization they had selected. I told her I would not only match the fee, I would also, if they were pleased with our training, lower it five percent if they would commit to have our firm be their vendor of choice annually.

This fee concession helped us to earn the business and paid big dividends during subsequent years. In fact, this client stayed with us for four consecutive years. Thanks to this business, our firm received good press in *USA Today*, the *New York Law Journal*, and the *National Law Journal*.

Here's the point: I was having a "lousy day." Suppose I had let the problem of the water seeping into my room sour my emotions? Suppose I had taken that "no" quietly, and filed it under "What Else Can Go Wrong?"

Always remember: *It's when you are at your worst point in the day that you must try your hardest.* And believe me, when this principle works to your benefit, it feels absolutely wonderful!

Courtship Tips

1. When it feels like life is caving in around you, stay positive.

2. Accept "no" as a red flag for providing your prospect with another way of doing business with you.

If You're Down, Look Up

There are days when courting business may seem like work. You may have planted a lot of seeds by sending prospects letters of introduction, attending networking events, and following up with telephone calls. When it comes to closing business, you feel like you're pulling teeth. The results have been nil most of the week.

When you find yourself in this type of situation, keep your chin up as you continue to keep your follow-up momentum high. Recognize that if you keep planting seeds, the leads and closings will happen. The only unknown factor is *when*.

While you may not be able to control the *when*, what you can control is keeping your name in front of prospects and existing clients regularly. Let prospects see you as *wanting* rather than *needing* their business. Whatever you do, avoid looking desperate. Keep your positive mental attitude high as you continue to court prospects. Recognize that timing is everything. In time, the consistency you've displayed in keeping your name in front of prospects will in fact grow into client relationships.

Courtship Tips

1. Keep your positive mental attitude high as you are courting prospects.

2. Broadcast the message that you *want* business—rather than that you *need* it.

Belief Makes Things Happen

We all know that seeing is believing. However, do you know that believing is seeing? In other words, you must walk, talk, and write as though the relationship you are trying to bring into existence is in the process of being established. One way to do this is by substituting the word "if" with "when." For example, instead of "*If* you decide to use our service...," say "*When* the time is right to establish a working relationship...." Say it confidently!

By using words of confidence when you speak, you will both subconsciously and consciously convince yourself and your prospect that it's only a matter of time before you work together. And guess what? You'll be right!

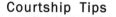

Courtship Tips

1. You have to know where you are going in order to get there. Identify the organizations where you want to do business.

2. Believing is seeing. Visualize the prospect companies where you want to do business. It will be the first step to acquiring them.

3. Use words of confidence. How can prospects trust you unless you sound believable?

Own Your Success

Accomplished, courtship-focused rainmakers "own" their success. They set goals for the end results they want and then do what it takes to make their dreams a reality.

These rainmakers set daily, weekly, monthly, and annual mile markers for themselves. They recognize that success will only come to them when they are willing to own the goal and the outcome they desire.

Rainmakers take professional or personal setbacks as opportunities for reassessing their present life strategies. They bounce back quickly, knowing that time is money. Successful rainmakers ponder quickly rather than analyzing a situation to death. They know from experience that getting back on the courtship bandwagon is the only thing that will convert prospects into clients.

Courtship Tips

1. Set goals—and own them.

2. If you are going to go through the process, make it a successful journey.

3. When a setback occurs, analyze it to see how it could be prevented in the future— and then get over it!

First Expect Prompt Results... Then Demand Them

Successful rainmakers go above and beyond for their prospects and clients. They do what it takes to get the job done.

When these ambitious people are in the role of prospect or client, they expect the best rather than mediocrity. When they don't get the results within a realistic time frame, they either demand action or they take their business elsewhere.

Let me give you an example of taking action. A friend of mine who lives in the Midwest decided to subscribe to the weekend delivery of a national newspaper whose name I will not mention. Two weeks after placing her online subscription, she still had not received the newspaper. She called the toll-free number and spoke with a call center operator. The person informed her that she had an undeliverable address. My friend explained to the operator that her neighbors who lived three houses away on a street around the corner have been receiving their newspaper for the past four months.

The operator requested a telephone number where my friend could be reached within 24 hours by the service center manager in her area. Forty-eight hours later, my friend once again called this newspaper's subscription line. Once again she explained the situation and was promised a call back within 24 hours. She explained that she had heard that story during a past conversation and asked to speak to a supervisor who would instill a sense of urgency to what should be a very simple solution.

The supervisor told her that he would send the local service center manager an e-mail marked urgent requesting that my friend be contacted promptly. My friend explained that she wanted action and would call back every three hours until she was assured that the newspaper would be on her driveway the following Saturday morning.

Three hours later, my feisty friend placed yet another call to the supervisor informing him that she was still awaiting a telephone call. The supervisor realized that she meant business and offered my friend the name and telephone number of an independent carrier. You guessed it. Two voice-mail messages and one telephone call later, my friend was assured that she would have the newspaper delivered the following weekend.

Why would something so simple take such energy? Frequently you find rote behavior in call center operators and even some supervisors. While it would have been great to take business elsewhere, these people were "the source" for beginning this newspaper subscription.

When developing relationships with vendors, look for those who work as though their salaries depend on it. Otherwise, they do not deserve your business. When you find yourself in the same situation as my friend by only having one source as your point of contact, do what it takes to get the job done.

Courtship Tips

1. Expect prompt results.

2. Evaluate prospective vendors according to this standard.

3. Let your own vendors know that you expect them to do what it takes to get the job done.

Tolerance Breeds Incompetence

When you're being courted by service providers, set your expectations high and keep them there. Expect your service providers to give the same commitment and attention to detail you give to your prospects and existing clients.

Continued tolerance of vendor errors breeds incompetence. Mistakes should be a learning experience, and they should happen only once. Accept excuses only if the situation is remedied promptly and does not recur.

Let me give you an example of an experience I had at what is considered to be a very respectable firm. I had the same investment counselor for more than 10 years. My advisor remained very accessible through phone and e-mail contact. I recognized that in order for her to work "on" business, she needed to delegate the "in" business transactions to her assistant. For that reason, her assistant was responsible for handling fund transfers and check reordering requests.

After three months of inconsistencies (not transferring funds, reordering checks I had already ordered), I realized that this administrative person was having more than her share of bad days. She was, in fact, incompetent. I began resenting having to work with her and would ask to speak directly to my advisor. The straw that broke the camel's back was when this administrative person did not tell my advisor that I called and requested a call back.

My advisor was very embarrassed about being represented by someone who paid so little attention to detail as this person.

I began wondering if I had done something to offend this administrative assistant. I asked my advisor if other clients have had poor experiences with this person, who was to be her right arm. She said, "You're not alone. This person made a mistake with another client that cost me $20,000 out of my own pocket."

I felt terrible for my advisor, yet I was relieved to know that the poor impression of this person was real.

In most organizations, documentation of continued inconsistencies would have been sufficient for giving this person a warning and then firing her. Instead, the only amends I received as a result of this poor soul's incompetent behavior was a telephone call from the director of the region with an "I'm personally sorry for the problems you've been having" and a "we're talking with her."

Two months later, similar acts happened again. I wrote another letter and got another "I'm sorry."

I lost trust in this firm. I realized that my advisor had no clout and the director appeared to only have enough authority to say "I'm sorry." I realized the person who was really at the masthead was the incompetent administrative assistant.

Because tolerance breeds incompetence, I decided to make my point very clear and changed advisors. I wrote another letter to the president of this world-renowned investment firm. In response, I got a call on the president's behalf apologizing for the poor experience I had with their firm.

Well, guess who was *still* in the driver's seat? The administrative assistant who was still making mistakes...and still fully employed. File it under "How to Hand Your Competitors Business!"

The moral of the story: *"I'm sorry" doesn't cut it. Results do.*

Courtship Tips

1. You are only as good as the individual(s) representing you.

2. An "I'm sorry" must be supported with results.

Hot Prospects, Cold Prospects

Hot prospects are the clients-in-the-making who have a need or willingness to develop a relationship with you in the immediate future. Cold prospects are those people with whom it looks like you have reached a dead end.

I strongly recommend that you develop and maintain a tracking list for both groups. When someone who was perceived as a hot prospect becomes a cold one, close the loop by sending the person a summary of the last communication you had. Document it in your tracking system and transfer it to your cold prospect list.

Many people throw away the time they spend with what looks like a no-close piece of business. They often find, however, that months and even years later, the prospect returns with a piece of business.

A cold prospect tracking system can allow you to win lots of new business easily by simply placing a phone call or sending a letter reviewing past communication and attempting to pick up where you left off. Forget about what happened three months ago. Ask the person what you can do to service his or her needs *today!*

5-24-04	**Chamber of Commerce**	212-555-1212	Jane Smith

123 Erie Avenue, New York, NY 10019

jane.smith@cofc.org

Sent an e-mail introduction to Jane after visiting with Barbara.

E-mailed the topics, along with the evaluation summary from the local chamber of commerce.

Mailed the originals to Jane, along with a copy of the information packet and blue 101 ways.

Added Jane to the corporate excel list to receive the Tip of the Month

Offered a specific amount if they decided to schedule a program the week of February 7 when we will be in the area working with other clients.

6-3-04 Spoke with Annie. Offered February 8. She mentioned that they do morning and afternoon sessions.

Quoted a specific amount per session for multiple programs.

Sent a follow-up letter to Jane.

Marked the calendar to call Jane on June 14 to learn how they would like to proceed.

6-16-04 E-mailed Jane to learn if they would like to reserve a program in February 2005 when we will be in the area.

Jane contacted our firm to let us know that we will be unable to work together this year.

Sent a follow-up letter to Jane and Barbara to let them know we remain only one telephone call or e-mail away when the time is right to work together.

Hot Prospect

6-21-04	**XXX Architects** 770-555-1212 Roger Manheim

423 Brown Street, Atlanta, GA 30328

rmanheim@xxx.com

Mr. Manheim contacted us about being part of their national sales meeting in 2005.

Approximately 400 individuals would take part in three consecutive programs. Client would be responsible for three nights of lodging (three trainers), meals, and ground transportation.

E-mailed a proposal to Mr. Manheim. We will hold January 8, 2005.

Sent the proposal to Mr. Manheim via FedEx with two copies of the blue 101 ways. (One copy is for the chairman of the board.)

Added Mr. Manheim and the chairman of the board to the Tip of the Month list.

6-29-04   E-mailed Mr. Manheim to see if he would like to secure January 8, 2005.

7-9-04   Susan called on behalf of Mr. Manheim. Susan's number is 770-555-1212; ext. 2.

7-16-04   Hold August 31 from 11:30 a.m.–1:30 p.m. for their team. Call Susan on July 23 to get additional information about an agenda for the pilot program.

8-31-04   Met with Mr. Manheim and the national sales team.

Secured Sunday, January 9, 2005, to work with their team.

Sent a four-way container of nuts as gift to Susan with the contract and copies of my books.

Cold Prospect

Courtship Tips

1. After and only after you've tried everything else, ask prospects those 10 magic words: *What is it going to take to earn your business?*

2. While you are waiting for prospects to become clients, act as their partner by referring business to them.

3. Check the temperature of your prospects every so often by asking what you could do better to serve their needs.

◆ How to Empower Your Prospects ◆

1. Try to get prospects to say "yes" to *something* at the end of every call or in-person contact.

2. Once you've tried everything else, ask prospects what it will take to earn their business.

3. Refer others to your prospects. By doing this, they will be appreciative and consider you their "partner."

4. Ask prospects and existing clients what you could do better to serve their needs.

◆◆◆

Role Reversal: When You Are Being Courted by Vendors

Charge us more—just treat us well.

No wonder the airlines of yesteryear have acquired *bankruptcy* as their middle name. While these airlines' ivory tower CEOs point a finger to a slowing economy affecting revenues, perhaps they should be a little more eager to hear *why* their customers are taking their business elsewhere.

These airlines are actually encouraging customers to do business with other airlines because of the voice-mail jail on their reservation lines. One airline in particular that was (note the past participle) my absolute favorite for the last 20 years lost my vote when they introduced automated voice mail that actually *discourages* your pressing zero to speak with a live human being. When you do press zero, the voice-mail android is prompted to apologize, saying she did not understand, and then asks you to repeat what you said—even though you "said" nothing.

Once you pound zero four or five times (a great stress release, yet hard on the phone), a real live agent answers. If you are fortunate enough to be a frequent flyer of that airline and give your number identifying you to the agent, the person will tell you that you will need to be transferred (what a perk!) to a special desk. That means your call will go back into a queue until an agent at your frequent flyer desk becomes available.

Hi-tech is nice, however hi-touch is what this airline has forgotten. The few times we want to talk to live human beings, they should be accessible for us rather than creating frustration with automated devices. If they don't modify their systems soon, they won't have to do so—because their formerly loyal customers will have chosen their competition as their airline of choice.

Courtship Tips

1. Make a positive first impression with callers by giving them access to a live human being first and automation second.

2. Recognize that business systems are only as good as what the majority of callers like.

3. Listen to prospect and client complaints rather than looking for ways to screen them out. These comments may be the last words you will hear from them before they do business with your competitor.

Conclusion

Advice From Seasoned Rainmakers

Manuel Gomez, Chief of Education and Training, Wright-Patterson Air Force Base

Recommendations for developing and maintaining business relationships:

Apply the "3-Gs" for successful relationships:

1. Get their attention (be original and recognizable).
2. Gain their trust (be honest and loyal).
3. Give of yourself (be committed and consistent).

Strategy for rainmakers to outclass their competition:

Apply the "3-Gs" for outclassing the competition:

1. Grab the opportunity.
2. Govern the situation.
3. Guarantee (and deliver) first-class results.

How to differentiate yourself from the competition:

Apply the "3-Gs" for making a difference:

1. Get involved (learn everything about the task/goal/expectation).
2. Generate (make it your own and get results).
3. Groom (prepare for the next challenge and develop your protégé).

Silvia L. Coulter, Chief Marketing and Business Development Officer
Dorsey & Whitney LLP

Recommendations for developing and maintaining business relationships:

"Keep in touch with everyone you've ever known. You never now who they know and who will recommend you to a colleague or hire you themselves."

"Building business is about building relationships. Those who do this well will reap the rewards down the road."

Strategy for rainmakers to outclass their competition:

"Remember that everyone's client is someone else's prospect."

How to differentiate yourself from the competition:

"Help prospects and clients achieve their business goals by introducing them to people with whom they may do business. It's a great way to demonstrate that you understand their business."

Ziad Khoury, President
The Khoury Group; Khoury Consulting, Inc.; and Khoury Claims Services

Recommendations for developing and maintaining business relationships:

"Know your product, believe in it, and articulate what's in it for the customer. Understand that at the end of every day, this is a business relationship. Developing and maintaining it will always depend on the dollars you help bring to the customer, as well as the quality of service you provide."

Strategy for rainmakers to outclass their competition:

"Information is power. Learn from both your successes and mistakes. Stay away from a generic, robotic presentation.

How to differentiate yourself from the competition:

"Technically, if you can identify every conceivable objection a customer may have and then directly or indirectly address it, you will close the deal 100 percent of the time."

Tramm Hudson, Senior Vice President
RBC Centura

Recommendations for developing and maintaining business relationships:

"Develop a knack for remembering names."

"Watch *The Godfather* again—focus on favors and relationships."

"Help a guy when he is down."

Strategy for rainmakers to outclass their competition:

"Remember to send thank-you notes for even the small courtesies."

For More Information

Do you have a business development question that was not addressed in this book? You can e-mail me at businesscourtship@ateaseinc.com.

Or you can write to me at:

At Ease Inc.

9056 Montgomery Road

Cincinnati, OH 45242

You may also have your questions answered by calling my hot line at (800) 873-9909. You can be assured of a prompt response.

AT·EASE·INC·

BUSINESS PROTOCOL & ETIQUETTE

Business Development HOTLINE

DO YOU HAVE A QUESTION ABOUT COURTING BUSINESS ON:
- The Most Effective Way For Contacting Prospects
- Why Prospects Have To See Things Seven Times To React?
- How To Differentiate Yourself From Your Competition?
- The Art Of Turning A "No" Today Into A "Yes" Tomorrow

E-Mail Your Questions To: businesscourtship@ateaseinc.com
or Call Our U.S. Domestic Hotline At (800) 873-9909
Or Fax Your Questions To (513) 241-8701
Visit Our Website At: www.ateaseinc.com
9056 Montgomery Road • Cincinnati, Ohio 45242

Index

About the Author

Ann Marie Sabath is the president of At Ease Inc., an 18-year-old firm specializing in domestic and international business etiquette programs. In addition to *Courting Business,* she is also the author of *Business Etiquette in Brief; Business Etiquette: 101 Ways to Conduct Business With Charm and Savvy; International Business Etiquette: Asia and the Pacific Rim; International Business Etiquette: Europe;* and *International Business Etiquette: Latin America.* Her sixth book, *Beyond Business Casual: What to Wear to Work if You Want to Get Ahead,* was released in April 2000 and made the front page of *USA Today* on June 27, 2000. Most recently, Sabath's rudeness reduction campaign was recognized in the March 1st issue of *Forbes* and in the May 2004 issue of *INC.*

Sabath's international and domestic etiquette concepts have been featured in the *Wall Street Journal*, *USA Today*, and Delta Airlines' *Sky* magazine. They also have been recognized on *The Oprah Winfrey Show* and *20/20.*

Since 1987, Sabath and her staff have trained more than 50,000 individuals representing the business, industry, government, and educational sectors in how to gain the competitive edge. Her "Strategies for Accelerating Business Relationships," "10 Key Ways For Enhancing Your Global Savvy," "Polish That Builds Profits," and "Business Etiquette: The Key to Effective Services and Enhancing Your Professional Style" programs have been presented to individuals representing American Express; EMC Corporation; New Balance Athletic Shoe; Fidelity Investments; Citigroup; Fleet; Cadwalader, Wickersham & Taft; Clifford Chance; Proskauer Rose; Marriott International; Andersen Corporation; Deloitte & Touche; MIT; Columbia University; and Miami University, among others.

In 1992, At Ease Inc., became an international firm by licensing its concept in Taiwan. In 1998, this firm also established its presence in Egypt, Australia, and Slovakia by certifying individuals in these countries.